THEOLOGICAL REFLECTIONS FROM THE SOUTH

Jesus in Africa

The Christian Gospel
in African History and Experience

To Prof. Bigelow,

In appreciation and
in partnership in todness.

[signature]

THEOLOGICAL REFLECTIONS FROM THE SOUTH

Titles forthcoming in the series

Kä Mana
Mercy Oduyoye
Lamin Sanneh
Jean-Marc Elà

Jesus in Africa

The Christian Gospel
in African History and Experience

Kwame Bediako

Introduction by
Hans Visser and Gillian Bediako

regnum
africa

Copyright © Kwame Bediako 2000

First published 2000 by
Editions Clé and Regnum Africa
in association with
Paternoster Publishing, P.O. Box 300, Carlisle, Cumbria CA3 0QS, U.K
and
P.O. Box 1047, Waynesboro, GA 30830-2047, U.S.A.

Editions Clé, B.P. 1501, Yaoundé, Cameroun
Regnum Africa (P.O. Box 76, Akropong-Akuapem, Ghana)
is part of Regnum Books International, a Two-Thirds World publishing company for
the International Fellowship of Evangelical Mission Theologians (INFEMIT),
formed of the African Theological Fellowship, the Latin American Theological
Fraternity and Partnership in Mission Asia.
P.O. Box 70, Oxford, OX2 6HB, UK
Jose Marmol 1734, 1602 Florida, Buenos Aires, Argentina
Post Bag No. 21, Vasant Vihar, New Delhi 110057, India
17951 Cowan, Irvine, California 92714, USA

03 02 01 00   7 6 5 4 3 2 1

The right of Kwame Bediako to be identified as the Author of this Work
has been asserted by him in accordance with Copyright, Designs
and Patents Act 1988.

British Library Cataloguing in Publication Data
A catalogue record for this book is available from the British Library

ISBN (Clé) 2-7235-0610-X
ISBN (Regnum) 1-870345-34-7

Typeset by Regnum Africa
and printed and bound by
Academe Art & Printing Services at Selangor, Malaysia.

Contents

(The chapters from Christianity in Africa *are reproduced in this abridged
form with the permission of Edinburgh University Press.)*

INTRODUCTION
Hans Visser with Gillian Bediako

Christ has been presented as the answer to the questions a white man would ask, the solution to the needs that Western man would feel, the Saviour of the world of the European world-view, the object of the adoration and prayer of historic Christendom. But if Christ were to appear as the answer to the questions that Africans are asking, what would he look like? (*The Primal Vision, Christian Presence amid African Religion*, 1963, p.16

This comment of J. V. Taylor is an appropriate introduction to this collection of articles by Professor Kwame Bediako. For it has been a major concern of his scholarly and pastoral ministry to investigate the question Taylor raises, in the full conviction that God speaks into the African context in African idiom, and that it is through hearing in African mother-tongues 'the great things that God has done' (Acts 2:11), that African theology emerges to edify not only the African Church but the Church world-wide. Before introducing this representative selection, we give a brief outline of his life, as the key to understanding his ideas.

Kwame Bediako was born on 7 July 1945 in Accra, the capital of Ghana, into a nominally Presbyterian family. He had his secondary education at the Mfantsipim School in Cape Coast, where Kofi Annan, the present Secretary General of the United Nations, was a few years his senior. He studied French at the University of Ghana, Legon. He received a scholarship for post-graduate studies at the University of Bordeaux. There he majored in modern French literature and African literature in French, gaining his doctorate degree in 1973.

Before he left for France in 1969, his father demonstrated his concern by taking his name to a shrine to ask for protection for his son during his studies abroad. At that time the Christian faith meant little to Kwame. He kept aloof from meetings of Christians and even actively disputed Christian claims with Christian student friends, until in 1970, in Bordeaux, France, he was collared, like Saul on his way to Damascus. Taking a shower one day, the fact that Christ is the Truth, the integrating principle of life as well as the key to true intellectual coherence, for himself and for the whole world, was impressed upon him with irresistible force. It took him some time to find a Bible, which he then read through several times.

In Bordeaux also he met Gillian from Blackburn, England, whom he married in 1973. Their marriage has been blessed with two sons. When he returned to Ghana in 1976, his father proposed to thank the shrine-spirit for his safe return. Kwame explained to him that he had come to understand that it was Jesus who protected him. His father replied, 'If Christ protects you now, that's fine. We do not need to go to the shrine.' Then Kwame said, 'He protects you too, father. He is the wall surrounding us.' Some years later, his father was soundly converted to Christ before he passed away in February 1999 at the age of 84.

Kwame's conversion led him to the study of theology, first at the London Bible College, and later, following ordination into the ministry of the Presbyterian Church of Ghana (PCG), at the University of Aberdeen. Under the guidance of the missiologist and church historian, Andrew Walls, he completed his thesis in 1983, which was subsequently published as *Theology and Identity: The Impact of Culture upon Christian Thought in the Second Century and Modern Africa* (1992). In this study he examines how four Church Fathers in the second and third centuries argued for the Christian faith in Greco-Roman culture as an intellectual category in its own right that provided the interpretative key for relating the Gospel to that culture. Then he considers how in the twentieth century four leading African theologians from different backgrounds struggled with the question of being a Christian in the African culture of today. Different readings of the Bible and different personalities lead to a variety of answers. This book was nominated as a finalist for the 1993 Harper-Collins Religious Book Award.

Back in Ghana in 1984, he was appointed Presbyterian and Resident Chaplain of the Ridge Church in Accra (an interdenominational congregation). However, he and Gillian already had the vision of founding a research centre that would address itself to the study of the relation between Gospel and culture in Africa. This idea had been born in 1974 at the Lausanne Congress on World Evangelisation. There he met other evangelicals, including Vinay Samuel from India and Rene Padilla, Samuel Escobar and Orlando Costas, from Latin America, who were seeking fresh insight into the Christian Gospel from the context itself that would also be universally valid. They developed an informal association: the International Fellowship of Evangelical Mission Theologians (INFEMIT), a radical evangelical movement.

In Ghana at about the same time and quite independently, the then Principal of the Presbyterian Training College, Akropong, the Rev. S.K. Aboa, was planning to start a research library for Ghanaian languages, on the understanding that, to be meaningful, the Gospel must be translated into the language of the listeners. Only then can it become part of the culture. In the early 1980s, Bediako and Aboa met and found their visions merging: a research centre with a library that would specialise in African theology and language and culture studies.

This project received the endorsement of the PCG authorities and in 1987 the inauguration of the Akrofi-Christaller Memorial Centre for Mission Research and Applied Theology (ACMC) took place in the so-called 'Baslerhaus' in Akropong, the capital of the Akan kingdom of Akuapem, after the launching of the concept in Accra in November 1986. The Centre was named after a 19th century pioneer Bible translator of the Basel Mission, Rev. Johannes Gottlieb Christaller, and his 20th century Ghanaian successor, Dr. Clement Anderson Akrofi. At this Centre, courses and seminars in mission and spiritual renewal are organised for laymen and pastors, initially for the PCG only, but subsequently for other denominations also. It serves also as a retreat and conference centre. In 1998 the Centre was given the status of a post-graduate institution by the National Accreditation Board of the Ghana Ministry of Education.

Internationally the ACMC has become part of a number of networks. We have already mentioned the INFEMIT. The African network affiliated to the INFEMIT is the African Theological Fellowship (ATF), of which Kwame Bediako is General Secretary. A recent initiative of this association has been to develop a Masters programme in African Christianity, in conjunction with the School of Theology of the University of Natal, Pietermaritzburg, South Africa. This is a two-year course with teaching in two locations, in Ghana and South Africa, and with field research orientation in Kenya. The purpose is to provide training in theology in the African context that equips young scholars to find Christian answers to African questions. This course has the potential for training a new generation of African theologians, and for eventually attracting students from the West who are open to learn in and from Africa. It is open to both 'evangelicals' and 'ecumenicals', as the aim is to transcend European denominational barriers and the artificial borders between francophone and anglophone Africa. In 1998 Bediako was made an honorary Professor in the University of Natal.

Another network is the African Theological Initiative (ATI) that came into being in 1992. With initial assistance from the Pew Charitable Trusts, USA, this Initiative aims to raise the capacity and the quality of African theological institutions so as to help reverse the brain drain of theologians from Africa to the West. The ACMC is one of the institutions identified by the ATI as pacesetting, with the capacity to help other institutions develop.

Kwame Bediako has been a driving force behind these initiatives. He has worked tirelessly to build the ACMC and has received increasing international recognition for his work. The Centre has programme links with several institutions in Europe: the Centre for the Study of Christianity in the Non-Western World in the University of Edinburgh, the Oxford Centre for Mission Studies, and the Hendrik Kraemer Instituut in the Netherlands.

A former student of Andrew Walls, Bediako is impressed by the shift in the centre of gravity of world Christianity in our days, in which Africa plays a significant part. This development requires people who are committed in mind and heart to Africa and to the Gospel, who can enhance the process by which the Gospel takes root in the social, political and cultural soil. Several levels of translation are required if Christian faith is to be more than a superficial layer of varnish. People need to be trained to undertake this task of translating the Gospel into the idiom and thought forms of local cultures.

These are the issues that concern Kwame Bediako and shape his thinking and ministry in Africa. At the same time, he is convinced that the theology that emerges from the cutting edge of the interaction of the Gospel and culture in Africa has universal relevance and far-reaching significance for the global church. For this collection, nine articles or chapters have been selected and grouped around three themes: the experience of Jesus in Africa, theology and culture, and the role Africa plays in the history of Christianity.

The African experience of Jesus

In the first chapter, Bediako gives a theological appraisal of the prayers and songs of praise of Afua Kuma, an illiterate midwife, who expresses in her own language what Jesus means to her in everyday life. She does so with images that, translated into a shared language, come alive for Africans from different parts of the continent. 'Jesus, the grinding stone', 'the lion of the grasslands', 'the Big Tree', 'the Great Doctor'. The cross is the fishing net with which men are caught. Jesus is present in nature and at birth. He gives food. The sun and moon are his robe. These are images derived from nature, from the daily struggle for life, from the fight against powers of darkness.

Bediako shows how Afua Kuma links ordinary human experiences to Jesus in such a way that he takes on new meaning. This theology of the grassroots makes it clear that the Christian faith is not a western religion but an authentic African experience. It is the spontaneous theology of the open air, the market and the home, that must precede and undergird academic reflection. This approach is important to all who have been brought up on a formalised theology that dampens freshness and weakens vitality.

In African life the ancestors play an important role. They are the living dead who are present in people's lives. Ancestors provide identity and protection. Western mission ignored the ancestors and condemned the rituals connected with them. The result was not that the ancestors disappeared, but that they continued to appear in people's lives at significant moments, but separated from Christian faith and expression. In the second chapter, Bediako deals explicitly with ancestors and describes Jesus as the Ancestor from a biblical and theological perspective. Jesus fulfils and transcends the functions of the ancestor. The epistle to the Hebrews, a letter to Africans according to Bediako, provides the biblical undergirding for this perception of Jesus.

African religious reality is pluralistic. Traditional religions, Islam and

Christianity, exist side by side and in many varieties. Bediako sees similarities with the environment of the early centuries when the Apologists justified their faith in Christ as the unique Lord and Saviour. In the third chapter, he shows that Christ is the eternal Word, just as is the Qu'ran for Muslims. However, in contrast to the Qu'ran, Christ is the Word of God translated. His divinity is translated into humanity, humanity being the receptor language.

Three aspects of his life and ministry make Christ unique. First, the incarnation in which God becomes vulnerable man. Second, the Cross, in which God's will for reconciliation through redemptive suffering is expressed. Third, the Last Supper, where the communion with the Lord is celebrated in a human community that transcends all borders, nations and languages. Christ is the vulnerable one who accepted the way of the Cross. In doing so he shows himself to be in the line of the true prophets of the Old Testament and contrasts with Mohammed, who, when faced with similar circumstances, fought back. It is in this will to be vulnerable that Jesus is Lord.

Theology and culture

In the second part, African theology is the centre of interest. African theology charts its own distinctive course, because African religious experience and heritage, referred to by the generic term 'primal religion', provide the substratum. Africa has had its own knowledge of God. The post-missionary church, following Western missionary attitudes, did not pay much attention to this initially. According to John Mbiti, it did not have much theology or theological consciousness. Now, however, a process of rehabilitation of this religious heritage has begun. Kwame Bediako states that pre-Christian religious memories underlie the identity of African Christians in the present. The pertinent question is: what constitutes this past of African Christians? This theological question leads to the new method of taking the past seriously. In the 1970s and 1980s, the theological debate centred on continuity. Nigerian theologian, Bolaji Idowu, upheld a radical continuity, whereas another Nigerian theologian, Byang Kato, was convinced of a radical discontinuity. Most theologians took a middle position.

The 1990s saw new developments, including the use of authentically African categories for Jesus. This process led to a fresh appraisal of pre-Christian traditions. Agreeing with the Gambian theologian, Lamin Sanneh, Bediako considers the vernacular (mother-tongue) languages as essential vehicles of religious transition. The Gospel is translatable into the vernacular, for God speaks Twi, Swahili, Setswana. African languages are therefore capable of possessing a transcendental range. The pre-Christian religious cultures can be bearers of divine revelation and indigenous languages are adequate for conceiving and expressing the Christian message. This method is relevant for Europe also. Yet there, the primal religious traditions have been almost completely erased. In Africa, religion remains part of African consciousness as a whole. Identity is tied up with it and so it relates more fully to everyday life, in contrast to the European secular self-understanding.

In the fifth chapter, 'Africa and the Fathers', Bediako amplifies this debate by comparing the second century with modern Africa. Common to both is the effort to integrate the existing culture into the light of the new faith. The second century was characterised by religious pluralism, just as Christians in modern Africa have to engage with the traditional religions of the African context. From the Church Fathers one can learn that it is possible to give a sympathetic interpretation of the religious past, including the religious past of Africa. The perspectives of these Church Fathers on issues of Gospel and culture have rarely been taken into account. Bediako makes it clear that culture itself may lead people to accept Christ. This view is diametrically opposed to the one that sets the Gospel and culture against each other, which has tended to prevail in the West and was imported into Africa.

In the sixth chapter, Bediako pursues further the question of the translatability of the Gospel. The translation of the Gospel takes place in a process of communication, interaction and refinement of theological understanding that gives rise to a new Christian idiom. Indigenous languages provide dimensions of perception that are non-existent in the English language. No Akan will pray to Jesus as 'Ancestor Jesus', but will do so to Jesus as 'Nana Yesu', which translates into English as 'ancestor Jesus'. The word 'Nana' has resonances that 'ancestor' does not. Bediako considers that the use of Nana is legitimate, drawing a parallel with the Christology of Paul who uses Greek categories to describe Christ, enabling the Gospel to take root in the Greco-Roman world. Justin Martyr also declared that Christ could be at home in the Hellenistic world. This does not mean that with the acceptance of Christian faith everything remains the same. A complete refiguration of the cultural heritage in Christian terms takes place, with room for a greater flexibility in vernacular Christology. Giving Jesus African titles, such as Doctor or Ancestor, enables Christ's song to ring out in many languages.

Africa and the history of Christianity

In the third part of this collection, Bediako concentrates on the significance of Africa in the history of Christianity. A most striking development in the 20th century was the massive numerical growth of Christian faith in Africa. At the first World Missionary Conference in Edinburgh in 1910, it was said that African 'animism' offered few starting-points for the preaching of the Gospel, and it was feared that Islam would become the dominant religion. Yet it was Africans of primal religious background who gave the greatest impetus to this growth. As Bediako continually stresses the importance of this world view, it may be helpful to indicate some common features: the close connection with, and dependence on nature, the awareness of spirits and powers, the ancestors, and the oneness of the physical and the spiritual. The human person is not an isolated individual but finds his place in a cosmic universe. It is apparent that Christian faith shows some affinities with primal religions, and at the same time is capable of being shaped by them. What is happening to Christianity now is therefore important for the West as well. Questions about human identity, community, ecological balance and justice, questions whose answers are sought by western theologians, are being solved in Africa in a way that would be difficult in the West at the present time.

Christianity has played an important role in African politics. At first this came through education, producing the first generation of nationalists who led African countries to independence. However, soon after independence, over much of Africa one-party states came into being, sanctioning dictatorial rule by leaders who aspired to be presidents for life. They sacralised their power by assuming the titles and roles ascribed to ancestors. One of the best-known of these leaders was Kwame Nkrumah, the first president of Ghana, who assumed the ancestral title, 'Osagyefo', meaning 'redeemer'.

In the 1990s, Christianity was faced with the even greater task of how to desacralise this power. Desacralisation does not mean obliterating the spiritual dimension, but introducing new concepts of power. Jesus was not inspired with a love for power, but with the power of self-sacrificing love. The non-dominating mind of Christ is the message of the Christian church for all in high positions who seek to 'show where power lies'.

In the final chapter Bediako shows how a new vision of church history is necessary, in which Africa needs to be recognised as a new centre of world Christianity. In Africa we have found that Christ has to do with visions, places, ideas and ways of relating, that the West does not understand. In this connection Bediako also mentions liberation theology. The theologies of the South point in a direction that implies the decolonisation of Christianity. It is no longer a Western religion but shows itself as truly universal. There is also a clear challenge to the Western church, in the words of John Mbiti: 'We have eaten theology with you, will you now eat theology with us?'

Kwame Bediako makes it clear that this new prominence of Africa in the world church at the end of the twentieth century and on the threshold of the third millennium, is not a call for African self-congratulation, but for sober reflection and faithful witness on the part of the African Christian church, a call that may be heeded or ignored. It is hoped that this collection of articles will contribute to stimulating that reflection and encourage faithful witness to the Gospel in Africa in our time.

Dr. J. J. Visser is Director of the Hendrik Kraemer Institute, in the Netherlands, and has collaborated with the author on several training programmes that link HKI with ACMC. Dr. Gillian Bediako is a senior staff member, as Documentation and Editorial Officer, at Akrofi-Christaller Memorial Centre, Akropong, Ghana, and is the Editor of the Centre's Journal of African Christian Thought.

I. The African Experience of Jesus

CHAPTER 1

Cry Jesus! Christian theology and presence in modern Africa

Modern Africa as a heartland of the Christian religion

We may perhaps take it for granted that with the publication by David Barrett of the *World Christian Encyclopaedia*, (Nairobi: OUP, 1982), many Christians have become accustomed to the phenomenon referred to as the modern shift of the centre of gravity of Christianity. The idea is that in our time, the heartlands of the Christian faith are no longer found in the Western world, but in the non-Western world; not in the northern continents, but in the southern continents of Latin America, Asia and particularly Africa. In 1900, 80% of the world's Christians lived in Europe and North America. Today, over 60% of the world's Christians live in Latin America, Asia and Africa. By AD 2000, there could be between 330 million and 350 million Christians in Africa. By any account, Africa has become a heartland of the Christian faith in our time.

In fact, Barrett had earlier published an article with the title, *AD 2000: 350 million Christians in Africa,* in which he argued, on the basis of his demographic projections, that by the end of the century, Africa might well 'tip the balance and transform Christianity permanently, into a primarily non-Western religion'(Barrett, 1970: 50). We can now say that this has happened. Christianity has become a non-Western religion; which means, not that Western Christianity has become irrelevant, but rather that Christianity may now be seen for what it truly is, a universal religion, and that what has taken place in Africa has been a significant part of this process.

I wish to dwell a little on this significance of Africa, because there is only one word that can truly describe the present status of Christianity in Africa as we approach the new century. That word is, 'surprise'; surprise, I suggest, in the fact that Africa has become so massively Christian at all.

For, at the start of this century, in 1910, when the World Missionary Conference met in Edinburgh to consider the 'missionary problems in relation to the non-Christian world', and particularly to seek ways in which the Christian Gospel might make a greater impact upon the world's religions, it was the primal religions of Africa, roundly called 'Animism'—a description taken from a man who was not particularly religious himself and who probably never met any of those to whose religion he gave the term—which caused the most concern. The general feeling was that there was 'practically no religious content in Animism', nor was there in it 'any preparation for Christianity' (*Missionary Message*, 1910:24). In fact, the official report stated: 'If things continue as they are now tending, Africa may become a Mohammedan continent' (Barrett, 1970: 39). No one then foresaw the emergence of a vibrant Christian presence in Africa, let alone the emergence of a distinctively African experience of Jesus Christ.

Christian Africa: the surprise factor in the modern missionary story

There is a further twist to this surprise element in modern Africa's Christian story. When the later important 'Africa' missionary conference met at Le Zoute, Belgium, in September 1926, it appeared that the missionary movement was now reflecting on, and learning from, its African experience. In fact, the conference was convened precisely because there was a feeling that the Edinburgh 1910 conference had not given adequate attention to Africa. Unlike Edinburgh 1910, which had had no African participant, Le Zoute included a number of African Christian leaders representing their churches and mission communities.

On the question whether there did exist any 'preparation for Christianity' in the African religious past, Le Zoute struck a quite different note from Edinburgh, by affirming that 'it has now become recognised that Africans have been prepared by previous experience for the reception of the Gospel and that their experience contains elements of high religious value'(Smith, E.W., 1926:16). But perhaps, more significantly, the conference also expressed unease regarding the calibre of the missionary personnel being sent to Africa, and their capacity for sustained impact. This led the conference to declare, as follows:

> Surely the day has gone when the best men could be picked out for India and China and the rest sent to Africa, as if any man or woman were good enough for Africa. The time for amateurs has passed—if it ever existed. Nothing is too good for Africa. (Smith, E.W., 1926:46)

The Conference even passed resolutions on the subject, recommending to mission boards, committees and agencies that they 'provide full opportunity and time to African missionaries, by means of recognised courses at home or on the field, to study native languages, customs and religion, that they may make an effective approach to the African mind'.

Valuable and important as these declarations at Le Zoute were, they are not as central to the story of African Christianity in the 20th century as they may sound. By the early decades of the century, the missionary movement had unleashed forces which would lead to a major Christian breakthrough on the continent, but it was a breakthrough which Western missionaries on the whole did not see because they did not expect it. Furthermore, the foundations for this breakthrough had been laid, in fact, by some of those 'amateurs', men of 'humble background and modest attainments' who, as Andrew Walls has shown in a most illuminating study on the subject, 'would not have been considered for ordination at home' and yet who 'in order to reach the mission field, or in order to be more effective there, set themselves to intellectual effort and acquired learning and skills far beyond anything which would have been required of them in their ordinary run of life' (Walls,1996:171-72).

Such a one was Robert Moffat (of Bechuanaland) who had been an Englishman's gardener in Cheshire before he became 'one of God's gardeners' as Edwin Smith called him in his biography; when Moffat experienced a spiritual awakening as a result of his association with Methodists, and subsequently felt the initial stirrings of a missionary vocation, his first thought was: 'I have never been to college; no missionary society will accept me.'

Another was Johannes Christaller (of the Gold Coast, now Ghana), son of a tailor and a baker's daughter; on returning to his native Germany after a distinguished missionary career, he would not be awarded an honorary doctorate by the Theology Faculty of Tübingen University because he had no university degree. Yet this is the missionary of whose work Dr. Noel Smith wrote in his doctoral thesis for Edinburgh University,

> Christaller's work achieved three things: it raised the Twi language to a literary level and provided the basis of all later work in the language; it gave the first real insight into Akan religious, social and moral ideas; and it welded the expression of Akan Christian worship to the native tongue. (Smith, N.,1965:55)

Scotland did better for Moffat; Edinburgh University awarded him a Doctor of Divinity!

There is therefore a further sense yet in which the emergence of Christian Africa in the 20th century was to be a surprise story of the modern missionary movement. By its deep and early vernacular achievement, that is, relative to Europe's own missionary past, the modern missionary movement had actually ensured that Africans had the means to make their own responses to the Christian message, and in terms of their own needs and categories of meaning. Already as from the late 19th and early 20th centuries, through a variety of factors including frustration with Western missionary paternalism and control, Africans had set about establishing what came to be called African Independent Churches (or African Instituted Churches in some of the more recent literature). Many of the earlier investigations of this phenomenon tended to focus on the sociological and political causes which saw them essentially, if not even exclusively, as protest movements; rarely were religious and properly Christian factors taken seriously into account. Only later did it become more widely acknowledged that the Christian Gospel in Africa had in fact 'had a liberating effect, setting man free, free from fear, fear of witches and the power of darkness, but above all conferring a freedom from an inner dependence on European tokens of grace or favour, to aim for higher things and a finer sensitivity' (Sundkler, 1976:318-19).

These were the words of one of the most sensitive of European interpreters of African Christianity, Swedish Lutheran Bishop Bengt Sundkler, in his book, *Zulu Zion and some Swazi Zionists*. And part of the process which I am referring to as the eventual realisation of the surprise element in the story of Christian Africa, I suggest, is reflected in the difference between his first pioneer study on the Independent Churches, *Bantu Prophets of South Africa* (1948) and the later *Zulu Zion* (1976). Having concluded in the earlier book that these 'syncretistic sects' as he called them, were 'the bridge over which Africans are brought back to heathenism', in the second he acknowledged a mistake in his previous interpretation.

> From the point of view of those involved, Zion was not turned to the past, but to the future and was their future.

The careers of William Wade Harris, John Swatson, Sampson Oppong, Joseph Babalola, Garrick Braide, in West Africa; of Simon Kimbangu in Congo/Zaire; of Isaiah Shembe in Southern Africa and several other dynamic African prophetic figures across the continent, a good number of whom were women, illustrate the point. None of them was commissioned by a missionary society, yet their ministries contributed significantly to the growth of mission churches, and all appeared in the same general period when the Le Zoute conference was lamenting missionary failures. All of this is sufficient indication that the making of Christian Africa in the 20th century has been 'to a surprising extent the result of African initiatives' (Walls,1989:5).

As Andrew Walls also noted:

> There is something symbolic in the fact that the first church in tropical Africa in modern times was not a missionary creation at all. It arrived ready-made, a body of people of African birth or descent who had come to faith in Christ as plantation slaves or as soldiers in the British army during the American War of Independence, or as farmers or squatters in Nova Scotia after it (p.5).

This was the first church in Sierra Leone, arriving there in 1792, the year of William Carey's *Enquiry into the Obligation of Christians to use Means for the conversion of the heathens*, urging British Christians to do something about getting the Gospel to non-Christians elsewhere in the world. Carey looked forward to the emergence of theologians, great Christian thinkers, indeed 'able divines' from among the 'heathens'. And yet the general expectation was that it would be the non-Christian monotheists, Jews and Muslims, then the 'civilised pagans', Hindus and Buddhists, in that order, who would lead the way. As far as 'barbarous and uncivilised heathens', that is, the Animists, were concerned, it was presumed they had more ground to cover. It was never conceived that heathen 'animistic' Africans would be among those who would make the most significant response to the Gospel message. The recognition that the forms of the religious life associated with the primal religions of the world, have in fact been the religious background of the majority of Christians everywhere, including the Christians of Europe, throughout Christian history, still lay in the future (see Turner,1977).

Africa and the future of Christianity

In our time, too, there has been much allusion to the marginalisation of Africa, following the end of the Cold War era, and in the expectation that Africa will hold a less strategic place in a world no longer dominated by the ideological rivalries between East and West, between capitalism and communism. However, it could be argued that in one particular respect, Africa will not be marginalised. That one area is the field of Christian theology and Christian religious scholarship generally.

I do not wish to make exaggerated claims for the African evidence; the present shift of the centre of gravity of Christianity to the non-Western world involves more than Africa. However, it can be argued that the African Christian field, not least because of its surprise element and its vibrancy, offers quite distinctive opportunities for fresh Christian theological reflection and for new understandings, for example, as to how the Gospel engages with culture. As Harold Turner has said:

> Here at the growing edges of Christianity in its most dynamic forms, the theologian is encouraged to do scientific theology again, because he has a whole living range of contemporary *data* on which to work. It is not that these dynamic areas of the Christian world are free from imperfection; but being full of old and new heresies, they need theology and offer it an important task. (Turner, 1974:177f)

Jesus of the deep forest: theology from where the faith must live

It is not my intention to pursue the argument about Africa's significance
beyond this point. What I propose to do, instead, is to present the evidence
of a theological articulation within Ghanaian Christianity—I believe it
exists elsewhere in Africa also—rarely mentioned in the usual discussions
about African theology, but important for our understanding of what has
happened and is happening in the life of many Christian communities in
Africa; it is the kind of evidence which helps to show how one is able to
speak of the Christian faith itself as having become a non-Western religion.
It is the evidence of what I call a 'grassroots' theology; some will call it an
oral theology, or even, a spontaneous or 'implicit theology' (Hastings,
1976:54) Yet it is, in its own way, also a reflective theology.

> Jesus is the grinding stone
> on which we sharpen our cutlasses,
> before we perform manly deeds.
> We have risen at dawn
> to take up our weapons of war,
> and join the battle.
> *Nkrante brafo*, You are the Sword Carrier
> *Okatakyi Birempon*: Hero Incomparable
> by the time we reach the edge of the battle the war has already ended.
> We turn back,
> singing praises.

> If you go with Jesus to war,
> no need for a sword or gun.
> The word of his mouth is the weapon
> which makes enemies turn and run.

> If we walk with Him and we meet with trouble
> we are not afraid.
> Should the devil himself become a lion
> and chase us as his prey,
> we shall have no fear
> Lamb of God!
> Satan says he is a wolf—
> Jesus stretches forth His hand,
> and look: Satan is a mouse!
> Holy One!   (pp. 17-18)

So runs a portion of the spontaneous adoration of Jesus by an illiterate Ghanaian Christian woman, Christina Afua Gyan, better known as Afua Kuma, a native of the forest town of Obo-Kwahu on the Kwahu mountain ridge in the Eastern Region of Ghana. There she lived, farmed and also practised as a traditional midwife. Her prayers and praises of Jesus are, of course, in her mother-tongue, the Akan language. But they have been faithfully translated into English by Fr. Jon Kirby, to give the reader a good indication of their depth of Christian experience conveyed in the thought-forms and categories of the Akan world view in her rural setting.

So, what is this illiterate Christian woman's place in African theology? Here, I believe, is an illustration of that spirituality which gives a clue to the vibrant Christian presence that we know of, and which forms the true basis of African theology; and which also provides clear evidence that Christianity in Africa is a truly African experience. For this is theology which comes from where the faith lives and must live continually, in the conditions of life of the community of faith, the theology of the living church, reflecting faith in the living Lord as present reality in daily life.

What is also immediately striking about Madam Afua Kuma's prayers and praises is how intensely they reflect a well-known and important feature of African primal religion, namely, a keen sense of nature, almost a 'fellow-feeling with nature', as Prof. Kwesi Dickson of Ghana has called it (Dickson, 1984:48-49).

In this setting of ubiquitous forces and mysterious powers, the Christian who has understood that Jesus Christ is a living reality, can be at home, assured in the faith that Jesus alone is Lord, Protector, Provider and Enabler. In the struggles and battles of life, the Christian discovers that Jesus goes ahead, and that, as *Okatakyi Birempon,* he alone is capable of fighting and conquering, leading his people in triumph. Satan may transform himself into a lion (*gyata*), or may equally become a wolf (*pataku*). These are no idle metaphors; in the world where 'the unseen powers are held to be active also in the natural order' (Dickson, 1984:49), a hunter or a farmer attacked by a wild beast may well consider that some spiritual agency or other is at work. And the Christian who has become conscious of spiritual warfare through reading the New Testament (Ephesians 6), needs no further demonstration of demonic activity. Jesus alone, the Holy One, is able to overcome the evil one, reducing him to a 'mouse,' so that 'we shall have no fear'.

Jesus blockades the road of death
with wisdom and power.
He, the sharpest of all great swords
has made the forest safe for the hunters.
The *mmoatia* he has cut to pieces;
he has caught *Sasabonsam*
and twisted off its head. (p. 19)

Mmoatia are supposed to be mysterious creatures with superhuman powers, that dwell deep in the forest; they are believed to be tiny, with feet that point backwards; suspending themselves from trees, they wait for the unwary hunter in the pitch darkness of the night. At their head, as their head spirit, is *Sasabonsam* with bloodshot eyes. His name has found its way in Akan Christian vocabulary to designate the devil. In the intensely concrete language of the Akan, 'Jesus has twisted off its head'.

> He is the Hunter gone to the deep forest
> *Sasabonsam,* the evil spirit
> has troubled hunters for many years.
> They ran in fear,
> leaving their guns behind.
> Jesus has found those same guns,
> and brought them to the hunters
> to go and kill the elephant.
> Truly Jesus is a Man among men,
> the most stalwart of men
> He stands firm as a rock.   (p. 19)

In this remarkable association of ideas, the one who has made the forest safe for the hunters is himself seen to have become a Hunter too, in order to deliver his fellows; and in this striking association of images, the Incarnation and the victory of the Cross are brought together and made meaningful in the defeat of the terrors of the African world, in both the invisible realm of *Sasabonsam* and his *mmoatia*, and in the visible realm of wild creatures like the elephant which, in rural Ghana, can suddenly attack a village and take away a child.

But this celebration of Jesus knows also a sense of history; for, '*Sasabonsam* the evil spirit has troubled hunters for many years.' But Jesus has now appeared, and is acknowledged where he was not known previously; and his defeat of *Sasabonsam*, while it is a living and abiding reality, nevertheless was a definite event in the past, but which now lives on in the local memory. So intense is this new consciousness of God in Jesus Christ that it makes all previous knowledge of God pale into insignificance:

> Our ancestors did not know *Onyankopon,* the Great God
> they served lesser gods and spirits and became tired.
> But as for us, we have seen holy men and prophets.
> We have gone to tell the angels
> how Jehovah helped us reach this place.
> Jehovah has helped us come this far;
> With gratitude we come before Jesus,
> the One who gives everlasting life.   (p. 30)

Jesus Christ, in bestowing everlasting life and this new knowledge of God, has also inaugurated a new era and constituted a new people, his people, bringing them into his Jerusalem, into his Zion, a Zion which is near at hand, and a place of security:

> The mountains of Jerusalem surround us
> We are in the midst
> of the mountains of Zion.
> Satan, your bullets can't touch us.
> If Satan says he will rise up against us
> we are still the people of Jesus.
> If Satan troubles us,
> Jesus Christ,
> You who are the Lion of the grasslands,
> You whose claws are sharp,
> will tear out his entrails
> and leave them on the ground
> for the flies to eat. (p. 46)

But the 'Jesus of the deep forest' is also the Jesus of the Gospels, the miracleworker who does the impossible, who triumphs over the obstacles of nature, who provides food for the hungry and water for the thirsty, who delivers from all manner of ailments and who bestows the wholeness of salvation. What is impossible for us is possible with him:

> Wonderworker, you are the one
> who has carried water in a basket
> and put it by the road side
> for the travellers to drink for three days.
> You use the basket to carry water to the desert,
> then you throw in your net and bring forth fish!
> You use the net to fetch water and put it into a basket.
> We ride in canoes on the water's surface and catch our fish! (p. 5)

Jesus reverses the terrors that threaten our lives, above all, the terror of death, 'so that we may be happy':

> *Tutugyagu*: the Fearless One [lit. unafraid of fire, firekiller]
> You have pulled the teeth of the viper,
> and there it lies
> immovable as a fallen tree, on which children play!
> *Adubasapon*: Strong-armed One [lit. ten arms rolled into one]
> You are the one who has tied death to a tree
> So that we may be happy.

Just as you have done in the days of old
today you continue to work your wonders!   (p. 7)

So the Jesus of the Gospel stories continues to manifest himself today, disclosing his power in the midst of the threatening conditions of existence, the images that describe these reversals taking on, sometimes, an uncannily startling quality:

You have put eggs at the lair of the egg-eating snake.
We went to look and the snake was lying dead!
You have left small chicks at the hawk's nest
And the hawk has fled, leaving the chicks behind.   (p. 7)

'This all-powerful Jesus who engages in marvellous deeds' is also:

Jesus, Saviour of the poor,
who brightens our faces!
Damfo-Adu [lit. Great Friend, Dependable Friend]
we rely on you as the tongue relies on the mouth.   (p. 5)

As dependable friend, Jesus ensures our wholesome growth:

The Great Rock we hide behind:
the great forest canopy that gives cool shade:
the Big Tree which lifts its vines to peep at the heavens,
the magnificent Tree whose dripping leaves
encourage the luxuriant growth below.   (p. 5)

Afua Kuma, as a midwife in rural Ghana, must have experienced the presence and power of Jesus in the course of the delivery of many babies:

When you heed the things of God,
you need not wear an amulet
to make your marriage fruitful.
A woman is struggling with a difficult labour,
and suddenly all is well.
The child, placenta and all, comes forth
without an operation. He is the Great Doctor.   (p. 14)

Jesus provides sustenance and meets the physical needs of his people; the provision that Jesus gives is depicted in a most delightful image, as an invitation to share in *his* resources:

You have spread your cloth
on the sea to dry;
a cloth for us to wear.   (p. 15)

And, as if an echo of the post-resurrection breakfast by Lake Tiberias in John 21:

You boiled your food in the stream
and when it was cooked
you poured some out for us to eat.
You use a needle to dig a wild yam.
You feed the army of the land
for three days,
and still some is left over.   (p. 15)

And the Jesus who provides so lavishly is also he who breaks down barriers between people, transforming 'enemies' into brothers and sisters, as he gives freely to all:

The famine has become severe,
let us go and tell Jesus!
He is the one who,
when He raises His hands,
gives even our enemies their share,
and our brothers bring head-pans
to carry the food away.   (p. 39)

So, he is the Lord and Saviour of all the nations, even though this truth is expressed in details relating to the landscape of the Kwahu mountain ridge of Eastern Ghana:

O great and powerful Jesus, incomparable Diviner,
the sun and moon are Your *batakari* [robe]
it sparkles like the morning star.
Sekyere Buruku, the tall mountain,
all the nations see Your glory.   (p. 6)

Sekyere Buruku recalls a local dcity associated with a prominent mountain in the Kwahu region. Most mornings, from the town of Abetifi, the highest inhabited point in Ghana, the mountain can be seen, erect and stately above the clouds; and here, from the 'power' of a local deity, the transition is easy to the glory and power of the true Lord of the land, come into his realm.

Amansanhene: King of the nations
He who brings nations together
milk and honey flow in His vein   (p. 23)

And all classes and groups of people find their longings met in him:

Children rush to meet Him
crowds of young people
rush about to make Him welcome.
Chief of young women:
they have strung a necklace of gold nuggets and beads
and hung it around Your neck
so we go before You,
shouting Your praises, *ose, ose,*
Chief of young men:
they are covered with precious beads
and gold pendants worn by princes.
They follow You, playing musical instruments.
Chief of all strong men: *Owesekramofohene* [lit. king of the valiant]
You have placed Your royal sword in our right hand
and the flag of victory in our left hand
while we lead You firing canons.
Chief of all chiefs
he says the chiefs are the wise men of the land
and let his judgment stand.
The one who lays his worries there
and says, 'Lord, judge for me'
is the only one that God can help;
God's wisdom sets him free.   (pp. 23-25)

Here is a picture of the Akan king, who, in traditional society, sits on the throne of the ancestors, receiving the homage of all his subjects at a high point of the year, as at the annual New Year *Odwira* Festival. But here the King is Jesus, the Chief of all chiefs. Yet the social and political relationships that sustain the community are not taken away, for the regular chiefs are in place—the 'wise men of the land'—and they give judgment; but their verdict is *his* judgment; for now the chief sits not on the throne of the ancestors to give judgment in their name; Jesus himself is King and from the unseen realm, God's word and God's wisdom set the accused free.

It is not surprising that in these prayers and praises of Jesus, all his honorific titles are such as were and are traditionally ascribed to the human sacral ruler. By giving ancestral and royal titles to Jesus, these prayers and praises indicate how deeply Madam Afua Kuma has apprehended the all-pervasive Lordship of Jesus, in the ancestral realm of spirit power, and in the realm of the living community under reigning kings. The biblical world is felt to be so close to the African world, that biblical realities take on a remarkable immediacy:

'Jesus! we have taken You out
and nailed You to a cross.
On a cross we have nailed You.
The cross is Your fishing net;
You cast it in the stream and catch men.
The cross is the bridge we cross over
to search for the well of His blood.
The blood-pool is there.

If it were not for the cross
we would never have the chance to wash in that blood;
the cross is the Christian's precious inheritance;
it brings us to eternal life.'   (pp. 35, 36)

And so the powers of the biblical world can also be experienced here and now, even in the uncertainties of modern African politics:

If you are in trouble with the government
you go and tell Jesus.
When you reach the court
they will say
'Go back home!'
No one will question you;
you won't have to say a word.   (p. 43)

There is no doubt that the christology of these texts is very elevated and stands as a significant illustration of an African response to Jesus marked by authentic African Christian religious experience and meditation.

African Theology: the quest and the discovery

I began by referring to the surprise element to its early Western interpreters in the African Christian story of this century. But the surprise would apply equally, in my view, to some of its later African interpreters. For, how else may we account for the curious fact that when the 'quest for an African theology' was launched by Africa's academic theologians in the late 1950s and early 1960s, there seemed hardly any awareness that an African theology actually existed 'at the grassroots', the result of a truly profound

African sense of Jesus Christ as living reality in the African world?

Bolaji Idowu of Nigeria, the *doyen* of West African academic theologians in the 1960s, wrote in frustration, that whatever theology the African Church had was 'a prefabricated theology, a book theology...what she reads in books written by European theologians, or what she is told by Europeans' (Idowu, 1965:22-23). John Mbiti, from Kenya, perhaps the best known African theologian of his generation, went even further, suggesting that 'mission Christianity' had produced a church 'trying to exist without a theology'(Mbiti,1969:232) and 'without theological consciousness and concern' (Mbiti, 1972:51). Under constant flogging from a critical European public impatient with Africa, because it was largely without understanding of the continent, these and other pioneers of African theology saw it as their task to construct the prescribed theology. Yet in actual African Christian life, where the faith had to live, a deep apprehension of Jesus Christ had laid the foundations for an African theology that, on discovery, can be seen to be the only valid basis for a tradition of academic theology.

The clue to what happened lies not so much in the African genius in religion, as in the nature of the Christian Faith itself; in the 'infinite cultural translatability' of the Gospel (Walls, 1981:39). Unlike in Islam, where the word of Allah is fully heard only in Arabic, in Christianity, the perception of the word of God is achieved in our own mother-tongues (Acts 2:11). It is to the credit of the modern missionary movement from the West that, in contrast to the mission to Europe in earlier times, the history of modern mission could be written as the history of Scripture translation.

In Africa, the continent of language and languages, the significance of this has been far-reaching. For, as Lamin Sanneh has graphically put it, the import of Scripture translation and its priority in missionary work is an indication that 'God was not disdainful of Africans as to be incommunicable in their languages' (Sanneh, 1983:166). This, Sanneh goes on, not only 'imbued African cultures with eternal significance and endowed African languages with a transcendent range', it also 'presumed that the God of the Bible had preceded the missionary into the receptor-culture'. As, through the very process of Scripture translation, 'the central categories of Christian theology—God, Jesus Christ, creation, history—are transposed into their local equivalents, suggesting that Christianity had been adequately anticipated', they create, in indigenous languages, resonances far beyond what the missionary transmission conceived. The centrality of Scripture translation points to the significance of African pre-Christian religious cultures, not only as a 'valid carriage for the divine revelation', but also as providing the idiom for Christian apprehension, as anyone who knows the origins of African Christian names for God will understand. In contrast to what had happened in the earlier evangelization of Europe, in Africa, the God whose name had been hallowed in indigenous languages in the pre-Christian tradition was found to be the God of the Bible, in a way that neither Zeus, nor

Jupiter, nor Odin could be. *Onyankopon* is the God and Father of our Lord Jesus Christ; Zeus, Jupiter and Odin are not.

The wider implications of all this are enormous for our subject; in that the relatively early possession of mother-tongue Scriptures meant that many Africans gained access to the original sources of Christian revelation as mediated through African traditional religious terminology and ideas. Through these, Jesus Christ the Lord had shouldered his way into the African religious world, and was to be discovered there by faith, not invented by theology. It is because John Mbiti came to appreciate this fact that, nearly 20 years after his critical comments about the Church in Africa, quoted above, he could write as follows:

> The Christian way of life is in Africa to stay, certainly within the fore-seeable future, [and] much of the theological activity in Christian Africa is being done as oral theology ... from the living experiences of Christians. It is theology in the open, from the pulpit, in the market-place, in the home as people pray or read and discuss the Scriptures...African Christianity cannot wait for written theology to keep pace with it...Academic theology can only come afterwards and examine the features retrospectively in order to understand them. (Mbiti,1986:229)

Theology as witness

But to speak of oral theology, in these terms, may even be misleading, as though all that we are dealing with is an oral phase, a transition stage, on the way to the academic or written theology, which then becomes the real theology. Furthermore, the special factors which have led to the development of theology as we usually regard it, as essentially an academic discipline and intellectual pursuit, necessarily literary, and a near-philosophical endeavour that requires specialist technical knowledge and skills, could give us the impression that this oral theology is found in only non-literate circles. Instead, we ought to speak positively of oral, spontaneous, implicit or grass-roots theology, as theology which comes from where the faith lives, in the life-situation of the community of faith. Accordingly, this 'grassroots' theology is an abiding element of all theology, and therefore, one that it is essential for academic theology to be in touch with, to listen to, to share in, and to learn from, but never to replace. Indeed, academic or written theology cannot replace this spontaneous or grassroots theology, because the two are complementary aspects of one reality, and the 'spontaneous' is the foundation of the 'academic'. Without this vital contact with the spontaneous, grassroots theology, academic theology anywhere can become detached from the community of faith and so be not much more than an exclusive conversation carried on among the guild of scholars, and incapable of communicating life in Jesus Christ to others.

However, when the two aspects are working well, theology acquires its authentic character—as a task, not of scholars alone, but of a community of believers who share in a common context, and are committed to the task of bringing the Gospel into contact with the questions and issues of their context. Within this understanding of our missionary calling, the special significance of this spontaneous theology is that it liberates the academic theologian from the false burden of having to 'construct a theology' as if by himself or herself. For its part, academic theology has the important role of understanding, clarifying and demonstrating the *universal* and *academic* significance of the grassroots theology in the interest of the wider missionary task of encountering the world with the Gospel.

I believe that if African Christian theology retains and maintains a vital link with the Christian presence in Africa, it will be poised to contribute significantly to shaping the Church for the coming century by recalling for Christian scholarship in our time, the perennial challenge that it is mission and faith in Jesus as Lord that give birth to theology; and that the supreme task of theology is witness: to 'Cry Jesus!', so that men and women may know, and respond to, the love of God for the world, shown in Jesus Christ.

But the final word belongs to the inspiring woman theologian from rural Ghana whose prayers and praises of Jesus remind us that, in the final analysis, the whole of our Christian calling is to worship Jesus the Lord.

> It is not for His miracles
> or wonderful works alone
> that we are following Jesus.
> For in Him is grace and blessing,
> In Him is eternal life, in Him, peace.   (p. 35)

> He is the One
> who cooks His food in huge palm-oil pots.
> Thousands of people have eaten,
> yet the remnants fill twelve baskets.
> If we leave all this, and go wandering off—
> If we leave His great gift, where else shall we go? (p. 38)

References

Barrett, D., 1970: 'AD2000: 350 million Christians in Africa', in *International Review of Mission*, vol. 59, January, (1970), 39-54.
Bediako, K., 1986: 'The Missionary Inheritance', in Robin Keeley (ed.), *Christianity—*

a World Faith, (Tring: Lion Publishing).

– 1995: *Christianity in Africa—The renewal of a non-Western religion,* (Edinburgh/New York: Edinburgh University Press/Orbis Books).

Dickson, K., 1984: *Theology in Africa,* (London: Darton, Longman & Todd).

Idowu, B., 1965: *Towards an indigenous church,* (London: OUP).

Mbiti, J., 1969: *African religions and philosophy,* (London: Heinemann).

– 1972: 'Some African concepts of Christology', in Georg F. Vicedom (ed.), *Christ and the Younger Churches,* (London: SPCK), 51-62.

– 1986: *Bible and Theology in African Christianity,* (Nairobi: OUP).

The Missionary Message, 1910: *The Missionary Message in relation to non-Christian religions—The World Missionary Conference 1910—report of Commission IV,* (Edinburgh & London: Oliphant, Anderson & Ferrier).

Sanneh, L., 1983: 'The horizontal and the vertical in mission—an African perspective', in *International Bulletin of Missionary Research,* vol.7, no. 4, Oct (1983), 165-71.

– 1989: *Translating the message—the missionary impact on culture,* (New York: Orbis Books).

Smith, E.W. (ed.), 1926: *The Christian Mission in Africa—A study based on the work of the International Conference at Le Zoute, Belgium, September, 14-21, 1926,* (London: Edinburgh House Press).

Smith, N., 1965: *The History of the Presbyterian Church of Ghana,1835-1960,* (Accra: Ghana Universities Press).

Stine, P. (ed.), 1990: *Bible Translation and the spread of the Church—the last 200 years,* (Leiden: E J Brill).

Sundkler, B., 1948: *Bantu Prophets of South Africa,* (London: OUP).

– 1976: *Zulu Zion and some Swazi Zionists,* (London: OUP).

Turner, H.W., 1974: 'The contribution of studies on religion in Africa to Western Religious Studies', in Glasswell, M. & Fasholé-Luke, E. (eds.), *New Testament Christianity for Africa and the World,* (London: SPCK), 169-78.

– 1977: 'The primal religions of the world and their study', in Victor Hayes (ed.) *Australian Essays in World Religions,* (Bedford Park: Australian Association for World Religions), .27-37.

Walls, A.F., 1989: *The significance of Christianity in Africa* (The St. Colm's Lecture, 1989, Edinburgh, unpublished).

– 1991: 'Structural problems in mission studies', in *International Bulletin of Missionary Research,* vol. 15, no. 4, Oct. (1991), 147-55.

– 1996: 'The Gospel as the prisoner and liberator of culture', in *The Missionary Movement in Christian History, Studies in the Transmission of Faith,* (Edinburgh/ New York: T. & T. Clark/Orbis Books), 3-15.

– 1996: 'Missionary vocation and the ministry—the first generation', in *The Missionary Movement in Christian History,* 160-72.

CHAPTER 2

Jesus in African culture: A Ghanaian perspective

Christian faith and African traditional religion in retrospect

Christ has been presented as the answer to questions a white man would ask, the solution to the needs that western man would feel, the Saviour of the world of the European world view, the object of the adoration and prayer of historic Christendom. But if Christ were to appear as the answer to the questions that Africans are asking, what would he look like? (Taylor, 1963:16)

This telling commentary on the presentation of the Gospel of Jesus Christ in Africa was made by one of the more perceptive missionaries to Africa of our time and describes the general character of western missionary preaching and teaching in Africa since the arrival of missionaries on our continent during the 19th century. It raises a question that must be faced by African churches and African Christians of today who are convinced that Jesus Christ, as *Universal* Saviour, is the Saviour of the African world, and who feel that the teaching they have so far received is inadequate.

Yet the negative side of missionary history in Africa must not be exaggerated, for several reasons. First, the vitality of our Christian communities bears witness to the fact that the Gospel really was communicated, however inadequate we may now consider that communication to have been. There is always more to the 'hearing' of the Word of God than can be contained in the actual preaching of it by the human agents (Taylor, 1958). The Holy Spirit is also present to interpret the Word of God directly to the hearers. The mercy and providence of God override human shortcomings.

Second, African theological thinkers now share in the inheritance of the Gospel as the Apostle Paul proclaimed it, the Gospel that set the early Gentile Christians free from Jewish Christian attempts to impose the regulations of the Jewish Law (Acts 15; Galatians). Paul grasped firmly the universality of the Gospel of Jesus the Messiah, insisting that the Gospel includes all peoples without reserve. He gave Gentile Christians the essential tools for assessing their own cultural heritage, for making their own contribution to Christian life and thought and for testing the genuineness and Christian character of that contribution. For many years African theologians have refused to accept the negative view of African religion held by western missionaries and have shown consistently the continuity of God from the pre-Christian African past into the Christian present (Idowu, 1962; Mbiti, 1970; Setiloane, 1976). They have, therefore, like the Apostle Paul, handed to us the assurance that with our Christian conversion, we are not introduced to a new God unrelated to the traditions of our past, but to One who brings to fulfilment all the highest religious and cultural aspirations of our heritage. In this way the limitations in our missionary past need no longer hinder the growth of Christian understanding and confidence in our churches.

A further reason touches on the nature of African Traditional Religion itself, and its encounter with the Christian faith. The common western missionary view of traditional religion was that it formed 'the religious beliefs of more or less backward and degraded peoples all over the world', (Gairdner, 1910:139) and that it held 'no preparation for Christianity'. Yet in more recent years, it has been shown that Christianity has spread most rapidly in 'societies with primal religious systems' (Walls, 1978), that is, religious systems akin to African Traditional Religion. These societies are the Mediterranean world of the early Christian centuries, the ancient peoples of northern Europe and modern 'primalists' of Black Africa, Asia, South America and Oceania. This fact of history has led to the question whether there might be 'affinities between the Christian and primal traditions'. It shows clearly that the form of religion once held to be the farthest removed from the Christian faith has had a closer relationship with it than any other (Turner, 1977:37). Indeed, since primal religions have been the 'most fertile soil for the Gospel', it has been argued that they 'underlie therefore the Christian faith of the vast majority of Christians of all ages and all nations' (Walls, 1978:11). John Mbiti has repeatedly argued that Africa's 'old' religions have been a crucial factor in the rapid spread of Christianity among African peoples (Mbiti, 1976). They were a vital preparation for the Gospel.

This argument stands on its head the western missionary view of African religions and so opens the way for a fresh approach as to how we may relate Jesus as Lord and Saviour to the spiritual realities of our context.

Jesus as divine conqueror in the African world

On the wider African scene, John Mbiti has considered African understandings of Christ, drawn largely from evidence from the Independent Churches, as churches within which African Christians have been able to express more freely their experience of the Christian faith than in the mission-dominated or historical (mainline) churches (Mbiti, 1973). Though the distinctions between 'independent' and 'historical' churches are now less meaningful than they once were (Walls, 1979), Mbiti's articles indicate that there are characteristically African understandings of Christ.

First, Jesus is seen above all else as the *Christus Victor* (Christ supreme over every spiritual rule and authority). This perception arises from Africans' keen awareness of forces and powers at work in the world that threaten the interests of life and harmony. Jesus is victorious over the spiritual realm, particularly over evil forces and so meets the need for a powerful protector.

The second important point is that for African Christians the term 'our Saviour' can refer also to God and to the Holy Spirit. Jesus, as our Saviour, brings near and makes universal the almightiness of God. Thus he 'is able to do all things, to save in all situations, to protect against all enemies, and is available whenever those who believe may call upon him'. The humanity of Jesus and his atoning work on the Cross are in the background and Jesus is taken to belong essentially to the more powerful realm of divinity, the realm of Spirit-power. Though Mbiti considers this view of Christ as inadequate, he does stress that there needs to be a 'deeper appreciation of the traditional African world, whose grip is so strong that it exercises a powerful influence on the manner of understanding and experiencing the Christian message...'.

Jesus and the ancestors in Akan world-view

These considerations bring us near the heart of the problem of understanding Christ authentically in the African world. Accepting Jesus as 'our Saviour' always involves making him at home in our spiritual universe and in terms of our religious needs and longings. So an understanding of Christ in relation to spirit-power in the African context is not necessarily less accurate than any other perception of Jesus. The question is whether such an understanding faithfully reflects biblical revelation and is rooted in true Christian experience. Biblical teaching clearly shows that Jesus is who he is (Saviour) because of what he has done and can do (save), and also that he was able to do what he did on the Cross because of who he is (God the Son) (Colossians 2:15ff). Since 'salvation' in the traditional African world involves a certain view of the realm of spirit-power and its effects upon the physical and spiritual dimensions of human existence, our reflection about Christ must speak to the questions posed by such a world-view. The needs of the African world require a view of Christ that meets those needs. And so who Jesus is in the African spiritual universe must not be separated from what he does and can do in that world. The way in which Jesus relates to the importance and function of the 'spirit fathers' or ancestors is crucial.

The Akan spirit world on which human existence is believed to depend, consists primarily of God, the Supreme Spirit Being (*Onyame*), Creator and Sustainer of the universe. Subordinate to God, with delegated authority from God, are the 'gods' (*abosom*) sometimes referred to as children of God

(*Nyame mma*), and the ancestors or 'spirit fathers' (*Nsamanfo*). The relative positions of the 'gods' and the ancestors may be summed up as follows:

> While God's power surpasses all others, the ancestors would appear to tilt the scale in their favour if their power could be weighed against that of the lesser gods. After all are the deities not often referred to as 'the innumerable gods of our ancestors', the spokesmen of the human spirits? (Sarpong, 1974:43)

John Pobee has also underlined the importance of the ancestors in the religious world-view of the Akan as the essential focus of piety:

> Whereas the gods may be treated with contempt if they fail to deliver the goods expected of them, the ancestors, like the Supreme Being, are always held in reverence or even worshipped. (Pobee, 1979:48)

> By virtue of being the part of the clan gone ahead to the house of God, they are believed to be powerful in the sense that they maintain the course of life here and now and influence it for good or ill. They ... provide the sanctions for the moral life of the nation and accordingly punish, exonerate or reward the living as the case may be. (Pobee, 1979: 46)

Ancestors are essentially clan or lineage ancestors. So they have to do with the community or society in which their progeny relate to one another and not with a system of religion as such. In this way, the 'religious ' functions and duties that relate to ancestors become binding on all members of the particular group who share common ancestors. Since the ancestors have such an important part to play in the well-being (or otherwise) of individuals and communities, the crucial question about our relationship to Jesus is, as John Pobee rightly puts it: 'Why should an Akan relate to Jesus of Nazareth who does not belong to his clan, family, tribe and nation?'

Up to now, our churches have tended to avoid the question and have presented the Gospel as though it was concerned with an entirely different compartment of life, unrelated to traditional religious piety. As a result, many people are uncertain about how the Jesus of the Church's preaching saves them from the terrors and fears that they experience in their traditional world-view. This shows how important it is to relate Christian understanding and experience to the realm of the ancestors. If this is not done, many African Christians will continue to be men and women 'living at two levels', half African and half European, but never belonging properly to either. We need to meet God in the Lord Jesus Christ speaking immediately to us in our particular circumstances, in a way that assures us that we can be authentic Africans and true Christians.

John Pobee suggests that we 'look on Jesus as the Great and Greatest Ancestor', since 'in Akan society the Supreme Being and the ancestors provide the sanctions for the good life, and the ancestors hold that authority as ministers of the Supreme Being' (Pobee, 1979:94). However, he approaches the issue largely through Akan wisdom sayings and proverbs, and so does not deal sufficiently with the religious nature of the question and underestimates the potential for conflict. For if we claim as the Greatest Ancestor one who, at the superficial level, 'does not belong to his clan, family, tribe and nation', the Akan non-Christian might well feel that the very grounds of his identity and personality are taken away from him. It is with such fears and dangers, as well as the meanings and intentions behind the old allegiances, that a fresh understanding of Christ has to deal.

The universality of Jesus Christ and our adoptive past

We need to read the Scriptures with Akan traditional piety well in view, in order to arrive at an understanding of Christ that deals with the perceived reality of the ancestors. We need also to make the biblical assumption that Jesus Christ is not a stranger to our heritage, starting from the universality of Jesus Christ rather than from his particularity as a Jew, and affirming that the Incarnation was the incarnation of the Saviour of all people, of all nations and of all times. Yet by insisting on the primacy of Jesus's universality, we do not reduce his incarnation and its particularity to a mere accident of history. We hold on to his incarnation as a Jew because by faith in him, we too share in the divine promises given to the patriarchs and through the history of ancient Israel (Ephesians 2:11-22). Salvation, though 'from the Jews' (John 4:22) is not thereby Jewish. To make Jesus little more than a typical Jew is to distort the truth. His statement in John 3:43-44 that a Jew could have for father, not Abraham at all, but the devil, was outrageous from a Jewish point of view. What counts is one's response to Jesus Christ. In these verses we find one of the clearest statements in Scripture that our true human identity as men and women made in the image of God, is not to be understood primarily in terms of racial, cultural, national or lineage categories, but in Jesus Christ himself. The true children of Abraham are those who put their faith in Jesus Christ in the same way that Abraham trusted God (Romans 4:11-12). Consequently, we have not merely our natural past; through our faith in Jesus, we have also an 'adoptive' past, the past of God, reaching into biblical history itself, aptly described as the 'Abrahamic link' (Walls, 1978:13).

In the same way, Jesus Christ, himself the image of the Father, by becoming one like us, has shared our *human* heritage. It is within this *human* heritage that he finds us and speaks to us in terms of its questions and puzzles. He challenges us to turn to him and participate in the new humanity for which he has come, died, been raised and glorified.

The Good News as our story

Once this basic, universal relevance of Jesus Christ is granted, it is no longer a question of trying to accommodate the Gospel in our culture; the Gospel becomes our story. Our Lord has been from the beginning the Word of God for us as for all people everywhere. He has been the source of our life and illuminator of our path in life, though, like all people everywhere, we also failed to understand him aright. But now he has made himself known, becoming one of us, one like us. By acknowledging him for who he is and by giving him our allegiance, we become what we are truly intended to be, by his gift, the children of God. Our response to him is crucial since becoming children of God does not stem from, nor is it limited by, the accidents of birth, race, culture, lineage or even 'religious' tradition. It comes to us by grace through faith.

This way of reading the early verses of John's Gospel that echo the early verses of Genesis 1, from the standpoint of faith in Jesus Christ as *our* story, helps us to appreciate the close association of our creation and our redemption, both achieved in and through Jesus Christ (Colossians 1:15ff). We are to understand our creation as the original revelation of God to us and covenant with us. It was in the creation of the universe and especially of man that God first revealed his Kingship to our ancestors and called them to freely obey him. Working from this insight, we, from African primal tradition, are given a biblical basis for discovering more about God within the framework of the high doctrine of God as Creator and Sustainer, that is deeply rooted in our heritage. More significantly, we are enabled to discover ourselves in Adam (Acts 17:26) and come out of the isolation which the closed system of clan, lineage, and family imposes, so that we can rediscover universal horizons.

However, 'as in Adam all die...' (1 Corinthians 15:22), Adam sinned and lost his place in the garden. Where the biblical account speaks of the expulsion of man (Genesis 3), African myths of origins talk of the withdrawal of God, so that he is continually in people's thoughts, yet is absent from daily living in any practical sense. The experience of ambiguity that comes from regarding lesser deities and ancestral spirits as both beneficent and malevolent, can only be resolved in a genuine incarnation of the Saviour from the realm beyond. But trinitarian doctrine is preserved, for the God who has become so deeply and actively involved in our condition is the Son (John 1:18) whom to see is to 'see' the Father (John 14:15ff; Acts 2:38f), and this is made possible through the Holy Spirit (John 14:23).

Jesus as 'Ancestor' and sole Mediator

Thus the gulf between the intense awareness of the existence of God and yet also of his 'remoteness' in African Traditional Religion is bridged in Christ alone because 'there has been a death which sets people free from the wrongs they did while the first covenant was in force' (Hebrews 9:15). How does this death relate to our story and particularly to our natural 'spirit-fathers'? Some suggest that ours is a 'shame culture' and not a 'guilt culture', on the grounds that public acceptance determines morality, and consequently a 'sense of sin' is said to be absent (Welbourn, 1968; Taylor, 1963:166-69). However, in our tradition, the essence of sin is in its being an antisocial act. This makes sin basically injury to the interests of another person and damage to the collective life of the group (Pobee, 1979:102ff; Busia, 1954:207).

Such a view of morality does not resolve the problem of the assurance of moral transformation that the human conscience needs. For the real problem of our sinfulness is the soiled conscience and against this, purificatory rites and sacrificial offerings to achieve social harmony are ineffectual. Yet the view of sin as antisocial is also biblically valid: sin is indeed sin against another person and the community's interest. But human beings are the creation of God, created in God's image, so social sin is also sin against God. The blood of Abel cried to God against Cain (Genesis 4). The Gospel underscores the valid insight about the social nature of sin, but brings the need for expiation into a wider context. Sin is more than antisocial act; the sinner sins ultimately against a personal God with a will and purpose in human history.

Seen from this angle, the insights about Jesus Christ in the epistle to the Hebrews are perhaps the most crucial of all. Our Saviour has not just become one like us; he has died for us. It is a death with eternal sacrificial significance. It deals with our moral failures and infringements of social relationships. It heals our wounded and soiled consciences and overcomes once and for all and at their roots, all that in our heritage and somewhat melancholy history, brings us grief, guilt, shame and bitterness. Our Saviour is our Elder Brother who has shared in our *African* experience in every respect, except our sin and alienation from God, an alienation with which our myths of origins make us only too familiar. Being our true Elder Brother now in the presence of his Father and our Father, he displaces the mediatorial function of our natural 'spirit-fathers'. For these themselves need saving, having originated from among us. It is known from African missionary history that one of the first actions of new converts was to pray for their ancestors who had passed on before the Gospel was proclaimed. This is an important testimony to the depth of their understanding of Jesus as sole Lord and Saviour. Jesus Christ, 'the Second Adam' from heaven (1 Corinthians 15:47) becomes for us the only mediator between God and ourselves (cf. 1 Timothy 2:5). He is the 'mediator of a better covenant' (Hebrews 8:6), relating our human destiny directly to God. He is truly our high priest who meets our needs to the full.

From the understanding held about the spirit-world, the resurrection and ascension of our Lord also assume great importance. He has now returned to the realm of spirit and therefore of power. From the standpoint of Akan traditional beliefs, Jesus has gone to the realm of the ancestor spirits and the 'gods'. We already know that power and resources for living come from there, but the terrors and misfortunes which could threaten and destroy life come from there also. But if Jesus has gone to the realm of the 'spirits and the gods', so to speak, he has gone there as Lord over them in the same way that he is Lord over us. He is Lord over the living and the dead, and over the 'living-dead', as ancestors are also called. He is supreme over all gods and authorities in the realm of spirit, summing up in himself all their powers and cancelling any terrorising influence they might be assumed to have upon us.

The guarantee that Jesus is Lord also in the realm of spirits is that he has sent us his own Spirit, the Holy Spirit, to dwell with us and be our protector, as well as Revealer of Truth and Sanctifier. In John 16:7ff, our Lord's insistence on going away to the Father includes this idea of his Lordship in the realm of spirits, as he himself enters the region of spirit. It also includes the idea of the protection and guidance that the coming Holy Spirit will provide for his followers in the world. The Holy Spirit is sent to convict the world of its sin in rejecting Jesus, and to demonstrate, to the shame of unbelievers, the true righteousness which is in Jesus and available only in him. He is also sent to reveal the spiritual significance of God's judgement upon the devil who deceives the world about its sin and blinds people to the perfect righteousness in Christ. Our Lord therefore, entering the region of spirit, sends the Holy Spirit to his followers to give them understanding of the realities in the realm of spirits. The close association of the defeat and overthrow of the devil ('ruler of this world') with the death, resurrection and exaltation of Jesus (John 12:31) is significant, and the thought of the 'keeping' and protection of his followers from 'the evil one' forms an important part of Jesus' prayer recorded in John 17, aptly described as his 'high priestly' prayer.

The epistle to the Hebrews as OUR epistle!

Turning to the epistle to the Hebrews, it has often been assumed that the problem of theology in New Testament times was how to relate the Gospel to Gentile cultures and traditions. The meaning of Christ for Jewish religious tradition was thought to be relatively simple. The epistle to the Hebrews however corrects that error. The writer is aware that some Hebrews might be tempted to turn from the proclamation of the great salvation in Christ.

The clue to the epistle's teaching lies in its presentation of Christ. Hebrews is the one book in the New Testament in which Jesus Christ is understood and presented as High Priest. And yet, 'If he were on earth, he would not be a priest at all...' Though our Saviour obviously does and did fulfil a High Priestly function in his redemptive work for us, the problem arises when one has to justify that insight on the basis of Old Testament prophecies and anticipations. The fact is, 'he was born a member of the tribe of Judah; and Moses did not mention this tribe when he spoke of priests' (Hebrews 7:14). The view of Christ in Hebrews involves making room in the tradition of priestly mediation for one who, at the purely human level, was an outsider to it. Just as an Akan might ask, 'Why should [he] relate to Jesus of Nazareth who does not belong to his clan, family, tribe and nation?', so a similar question must have occurred to some Hebrews in time past and the epistle was written to answer that question.

The writer's approach is to work *from* the achievement of Jesus in the meaning of his death and resurrection, *into* the biblical tradition of sacrifice and high priestly mediation. In the process, the universality of the Lord from heaven as the Saviour of *all* people everywhere, forms the basis of the call to Hebrew people to take him seriously as *their* Messiah. Even more striking, the writer shows that the High Priesthood of Jesus is not after the order of Aaron, the first Hebrew High Priest, but after that of the enigmatic non-Hebrew, and greater priest-king, Melchizedek (Hebrews 7 and 8). Therefore, the priesthood, mediation and hence the salvation that Jesus Christ brings to all people everywhere belong to an entirely different category from what people may claim for their clan, family, tribal and national priests and mediators. The quality of the achievement and ministry of Jesus Christ for and on behalf of all people, together with who he is, reveal his absolute supremacy. As One who is fully divine, he nonetheless took on human nature in order to offer himself in death as sacrifice for human sin. Jesus Christ is unique not because he stands apart from us but because no one has identified so profoundly with the human predicament as he has, in order to transform it. The uniqueness of Jesus Christ is rooted in his radical and direct significance for every human person, every human context and every human culture. The value for us of the presentation of Jesus in Hebrews stems from its relevance to a society like ours with its deep tradition of sacrifice, priestly mediation and ancestral function. In relation to each of these features of our religious heritage, Hebrews shows Jesus to be the answer to the spiritual longings and aspirations that our people have sought to meet through our traditions.

Sacrifice

Sacrifice as a way of ensuring a harmonious relationship between the human community and the realm of divine and mystical power, is a regular event in Ghanaian society. It is easy to assume that the mere performance of sacrifice is sufficient, yet the real problem is whether sacrifice achieves its purpose. Hebrews gives us the fundamental insight that since it is human sin and wrong-doing that sacrifice seeks to purge and atone for, no animal or sub-human victim can stand in for human beings. Nor can a sinful human being stand in for fellow sinners. The action of Jesus Christ, himself divine and sinless, in taking on human nature so as to willingly lay down his life for all humanity, fulfils perfectly the end that all sacrifices seek to achieve (Hebrews

9:12). No number of animal or other victims offered at any number of shrines can equal the one, perfect sacrifice made by Jesus Christ of himself for all time and for all peoples everywhere. To reject the worth of the achievement of Jesus Christ on the grounds of race, ethnicity, and cultural tradition, is to act against better knowledge, distort religious truth, and walk into a blind alley, in the words of Hebrews, to court 'the fearful prospect of judgement and the fierce fire which will destroy those who oppose God' (10:27).

Priestly Mediation

If the quality of Jesus's self-offering in death sets his sacrifice above all and achieves perfect atonement, so his priestly mediation surpasses all others. Jesus had no human hereditary claim to priesthood (Hebrews 7:14; 8:4), so the way is open for appreciating his priestly ministry for what it truly is. His taking of human nature enabled him to share the human predicament and so qualified him to act for humanity. His divine origin ensures that he is able to mediate between the human community and the divine realm in a way no human priest can. As himself God-man, Jesus bridges the gulf between the Holy God and sinful humanity, achieving for humanity the harmonious fellowship with God that all human priestly mediations only approximate.

Yet his priestly ministry takes place not in an earthly temple or shrine, but in the realm where it really matters, where all issues are decided, in the divine presence (Hebrews 9:24). But his priestly mediation has done more than act 'on our behalf'. It actually ends priestly mediation by bringing into the divine presence all who by faith associate themselves with him. The meeting of the perfect sacrifice with the perfect priestly mediation in the one person, Jesus Christ, means that having identified with humanity in order to taste death on behalf of humanity (Hebrews 2:14-15), he has opened the way for all who identify with him to be with him in the divine presence (Hebrews 10:19-20). This unique achievement renders all other priestly mediations obsolete and reveals their ineffectiveness. To disregard the surpassing worth of the priestly mediation of Jesus Christ for all people everywhere and to choose ethnic priesthoods in the name of cultural heritage, is to fail to recognise the true meaning and end of all priestly mediation, to abdicate from belonging within the one community of humanity, to clutch at the shadow and miss the substance. The thrust of Hebrews is that such error is not only unredeemable, it is also utterly unnecessary.

Ancestral Function

Of the three features of our traditional heritage we are considering, ancestral function seems to be the one to which Jesus Christ least easily answers.

Ancestors are lineage or family ancestors and so are by nature ours. So the cult of ancestors may be said to be beyond the reach of Christian argument. If the cult of ancestors is valid, here is solid ground on which traditional religion can take a firm stand. It is precisely here that the problem lies. In what does the validity of the cult of ancestors consist? Since not all become ancestors but only those who lived exemplary lives and from whom the community derived some benefit, are not ancestors in effect a projection into the transcendent realm of the social values and spiritual expectations of the living community? Since traditional society views existence as an integrated whole, linking the living and the departed in a common life, such a projection is understandable. Yet the essential point is that ancestors have no existence independent of the community that produces them. The cult of ancestors provides the basis for locating in the transcendent realm the source of authority and power in the community and gives to leadership itself a sacred quality.

Strictly speaking, the cult of ancestors, from the intellectual point of view, belongs to the category of myth, ancestors being the product of the myth-making imagination of the community. To characterise the cult of ancestors as 'myth' is not to say that the cult is unworthy of serious attention. The term stresses the functional value of the cult of ancestors. For myth is sacred, enshrining and expressing the most valued elements of a community's self-understanding. The cult of ancestors as myth points to the role of the cult in ensuring social harmony, by strengthening the ties that knit together all sections and generations of the community, the present with the past and those as yet unborn. On each occasion of heightened feeling in the community—birth, outdooring of infants, initiation into adulthood, marriage, death, the installation of a king and celebration of harvests—the cult of ancestors forms an essential part of the ritual ceremonies that secure the conditions upon which the life and continuity of the community are believed to depend.

It is also important to realise that since ancestors do not originate from the transcendent realm, it is the myth-making imagination of the community itself that sacralises them, conferring upon them the sacred authority that they exercise through those in the community, like kings, who also expect to become ancestors. The potency of the cult of ancestors is not the potency of ancestors themselves; the potency of the cult is the potency of myth.

Once the meaning of the cult of ancestors as myth is granted and its 'function' is understood within the overall religious life of traditional society, it becomes clear how Jesus Christ fulfils our aspirations in relation to ancestral function too. Ancestors are considered worthy of honour for having 'lived among us' and for having brought benefits to us; Jesus Christ has done infinitely more. They, originating from among us, had no choice but to live among us. But he, reflecting the brightness of God's glory and the exact likeness of God's own being (Hebrews 1:3), took our flesh and blood, shared our human nature and underwent death for us to set us free from the fear of death (Hebrews 2:14-15). He who has every reason to abandon sinful humans to their just deserts is not ashamed to call us his brethren (Hebrews 2:11). Our natural ancestors had no barriers to cross to live among us and share our experience. His incarnation implies that he has achieved a far more profound identification with us in our humanity than the mere ethnic solidarity of lineage ancestors can ever do. Jesus Christ surpasses our natural ancestors also by virtue of who he is in himself. Ancestors, even described as 'ancestral spirits', remain essentially human spirits; whatever benefit they may be said to bestow is effectively contained by the fact of their being human. Jesus Christ, on the other hand, took on human nature without loss to his divine nature. Belonging in the eternal realm as Son of the Father (Hebrews 1:1, 48; 9:14), he has taken human nature into himself (Hebrews 10:19) and so, as God-man, he ensures an infinitely more effective ministry to human beings (Hebrews 7:25) than can be said of merely human ancestral spirits.

The writer of Hebrews, confronted by the reality of the eternal nature of Jesus Christ, falls back on the enigmatic Melchizedek of Genesis 14:17-20 for analogy; without father or mother, without beginning or end, he (Melchizedek) is like the Son of God (Jesus Christ). The likeness is only in thought. For Jesus has actually demonstrated, through his resurrection from the dead, the possession of an indestructible life (Hebrews 7:16). This can never be said of ancestors. The persistence of the cult of ancestors is owed, not to their demonstrable power to act, but to the power of the myth that sustains them in the corporate mind of the community. The presumption that ancestors actually function for the benefit of the community can be seen as part of the same myth-making imagination that projects departed human beings into the transcendent realm. While not denying that spiritual forces do operate in the traditional realm, we can maintain that ancestral spirits, as human spirits that have not demonstrated any power over death, the final enemy, cannot be presumed to act in the way tradition ascribes to them.

Since ancestral function as traditionally understood is now shown to have no basis in fact, the way is open for appreciating more fully how Jesus Christ is the only real and true Ancestor and Source of life for all mankind, fulfilling and transcending the benefits believed to be bestowed by lineage ancestors. By his unique achievement in perfect atonement through his own self-sacrifice, and by effective eternal mediation and intercession as God-man in the divine presence, he has secured eternal redemption (Hebrews 9:12) for all who acknowledge who he is for them and what he has done for them, who abandon the blind alleys of merely human traditions and rituals, and instead, entrust themselves to him. As mediator of a new and better covenant between God and humanity (Hebrews 8:6; 12:24), Jesus brings the redeemed into the experience of a new identity in which he links their human destinies directly and consciously with the eternal, gracious will and purpose of a loving and caring God (Hebrews 12:22-24). No longer are human horizons bounded by lineage, clan, tribe or nation. For the redeemed now belong within the community of the living God, in the joyful company of the faithful of all ages and climes. They are united through their union with Christ, in a fellowship infinitely richer than the mere social bonds of lineage, clan, tribe or nation that exclude the stranger as a virtual enemy.

Reading and hearing the Word of God in our own language

Once we discover that there is no valid alternative to Jesus Christ, the question is no longer: why should we relate to Jesus of Nazareth who does not belong to our clan, family, tribe and nation? but, how may we understand more fully this Jesus Christ who relates to us most meaningfully and most profoundly in our clan, family, tribe and nation? A helpful way of growing in understanding is to read and listen to the Word of God in our own languages.

In matters of religion, no language speaks to the heart, mind and innermost feelings as does our mother-tongue. The achievement of Christianity with regard to this all-important place of language in religion is truly unique. For Christianity is, among all religions, the most culturally translatable, hence the most truly universal, being able to be at home in every cultural context without injury to its essential character. For a Scriptural religion rooting religious authority in a particular collection of sacred writings, this achievement is remarkable. Its explanation must lie with Christianity's refusal of a 'sacred' language. With the exception of the dominant role of Latin in the European phase of Christianity and in some sectors of Roman Catholicism, Christianity has developed as a 'vernacular' faith. The significance of this has been most marked in Africa, where the early possession of the Scriptures in mother-tongue meant that African peoples had access to the original sources of Christian teaching, on the authority of which they could, if need be, establish their own churches. Each of us with the Bible in our mother-tongue can truly claim to hear God speaking to us in our own language.

The importance of this fact is theological. The Christian belief that the Bible in the vernacular remains in every respect the Word of God, has its basis in what took place on the Day of Pentecost, when the Holy Spirit, through the first Christian witnesses, spoke at one and the same time to people 'who had come from every country in the world' (Acts 2:5 GNB), each in his own language, causing them to 'hear the great things that God has done' in Jesus Christ (Acts 2:1-12). Hearing the Word of God in our own language is not to be sneered at and left to 'illiterates'; it is essential if we seriously seek growth in our understanding of Jesus Christ. A final illustration from the epistle to the Hebrews clarifies the point:

> When he had made purification for sins, he sat down at the right hand of the Majesty on high (RSV). After achieving forgiveness for the sins of mankind, he sat down in heaven at the right hand side of God, the Supreme Power (GNB). (Hebrews 1:3b)

If Akan speakers read their Bibles only in the English versions and neglect the Word of God in their own language, it is conceivable that they would dutifully participate in every annual *Odwira* Festival without ever realising that the traditional purificatory rituals of *Odwira*, repeated year after year, have in fact been fulfilled and transcended by the one, perfect *Odwira* that Jesus Christ has performed once for all, (Hebrews 1:3 in Twi: ọde n'ankasa ne ho *dwiraa* yẹn bọne no). Jesus has thus secured eternal redemption for all who cease from their own works of purification and trust in him and his perfect *Odwira*; that it is Jesus Christ *in himself,* (the Twi here—*ọde n'ankasa ne ho*—being more expressive than the English versions), who has become our *Odwira*. The *Odwira* to end all *odwiras* has taken place through the death of Jesus Christ.

References

Busia, K.A., 1954: 'The Ashanti', in Daryll Forde (ed.), *African Worlds – Studies in the Cosmological Ideas and Social Values of African Peoples,* (London: OUP).

Gairdner, W.H.T., 1910: *Edinburgh 1910. An Account and Interpretation of the World Missionary Conference*, (London: Oliphant, Anderson and Ferrier).

Idowu, E. Bolaji, 1962: *Olódùmarè – God in Yoruba Belief,* (London: Longmans).

Mbiti, J.S., 1970: *Concepts of God in Africa*, (London: SPCK).

– 1973: ''Our Saviour' as an African Experience', in B. Lindars and S. Smalley (eds.), *Christ and the Spirit in the New Testament* (Essays in honour of C.F.D. Moule), (Cambridge: Cambridge University Press), 397-414.

– 1976: 'The Encounter between Christianity and African Religion', in *Temenos* 12, (1976), 125-35.

Pobee, John, 1979: *Towards an African Theology*, (Nashville: Abingdon Press).

Sarpong, Peter, 1974: *Ghana in Retrospect – Some aspects of Ghanaian culture*, (Accra-Tema: Ghana Publishing Corporation).

Setiloane, G.M., 1976: *The Image of God among the Sotho-Tswana*, (Rotterdam: A.A. Balkema).

Taylor, John V., 1958: *The Growth of the Church in Buganda – an attempt at understanding*, (London: SCM Press).

– 1963: *The Primal Vision – Christian Presence amid African Religion*, (London: SCM Press).

Turner, H.W., 1977: 'The Primal Religions of the World and their Study', in Victor C. Hayes (ed.), *Australian Essays in World Religions*, (Bedford Park: Australian Association for World Religions), 27-37.

Walls, A.F., 1978: 'Africa and Christian Identity', in *Mission Focus*, vol.IV, no.7, Nov., (1978), 11-13.

– 1979: 'The Anabaptists of Africa? The Challenge of the African Independent Churches', in *Occasional Bulletin of Missionary Research*, Vol. 3, No. 2, April, (1979), 48-51.

Welbourn, F.B., 1968: 'Some Problems of African Christianity: Guilt and Shame', in C.G. Baëta (ed.), *Christianity in Tropical Africa*, (London: OUP), 182-99.

CHAPTER 3

How is Jesus Christ Lord? Evangelical Christian apologetics amid African religious pluralism

Introduction: The biblical records as the fruit of engagement

In many evangelical circles there seems to be an unquestioned assumption that the only authentically 'evangelical' way to affirm Christian convictions is to avoid a serious engagement with alternative viewpoints. Yet it is difficult to conceive of the formation of the biblical records of both Old and New Testaments themselves without theological engagement with the alternative viewpoints present in the contexts in which the biblical witness was being assembled.

To mention merely the prophetic witness in the Old Testament, it is hard to make sense of the intense struggles against Baalism apart from the reality of 'other faiths' with which the prophets felt called to do battle. In relation to the New Testament, it seems hard to conceive of the coming into existence of large portions without the deep religious and intellectual engagements between the Gospel proclamation and the various 'mystery-religions' and other alternatives, quite apart from Judaism itself, in the Graeco-Roman world of the time.

The point, then, is that serious engagement with such alternatives, seems to be inbuilt in the process of giving final shape to the very source-materials for Christian theological reflection.

My route to the problem

As an African evangelical Christian of the twentieth century, my awareness that a creative African evangelical theological tradition can emerge from a serious engagement with the religious world of African traditional religions, as well as with the spiritual and intellectual problems which they pose, has been nurtured in three ways.

The first has to do with discoveries made in the course of the work I did for my doctoral thesis, subsequently published as, *Theology and Identity— The impact of culture upon Christian thought in the second century and modern Africa,* (Oxford: Regnum Books, 1992). In that work, I brought together two eras and contexts of Christian history—the Graeco-Roman world of the second century and the post-missionary African world of the twentieth century—in an attempt to show the relevance of the insights and achievements of the one context for the other. The point was not that the problems and issues that faced Christian thinkers in the one context could simply be read off from the other. My approach was to select a number of Christian writers from the two eras, and to study their responses to enduring questions in the area of Christ and culture as far as possible within each writer's own world of thought and concerns. Only after studying each writer against the background of the ideas and forces that shaped the writer's Christian and intellectual career, did I then proceed to seek analogous correlations between the two contexts.

My choice of ancient writers was Tatian, Tertullian, Justin and Clement of Alexandria; my modern African writers were Bolaji Idowu of Nigeria, John Mbiti of Kenya, Mulago Musharhamina of Zaire [now Democratic Republic of Congo], and Byang Kato of Nigeria. As my study progressed, it became increasingly clear to me that the early Christian theology was relevant for the theological enterprise in modern Africa. There were similarities in the context of religious pluralism and an equally remarkable common concern to make sense of Christian identity against a background of inherited cultural and religious ideas that appeared to be far removed from the 'adoptive' biblical tradition. In addition, the ability of the early Church Fathers to cut through the considerable challenges that faced them, and to reach a point where they identified what Marcel Simon called 'the specific nature of Christianity', was highly relevant to the African situation. For the discovery of Christianity itself as a 'historical category' enabled them—against all the odds, and even against the anti-Christian intellectuals of the time, like Celsus—to vindicate for their Christian conscience a place to feel at home in the common culture that they shared with their non-Christian contemporaries. (See the chapter on 'Africa and the Fathers' for an elaboration of this argument.)

The second route to my conviction regarding the potential fruitfulness of a serious engagement with African Traditional Religions for a creative African evangelical Christian apologetics has to do with observations made by Archbishop Anastasios Yannoulatos at the September 1973 Ibadan Consultation on 'Christian dialogue with traditional thought forms', published in the proceedings of that consultation, *Primal World-Views—Christian involvement in dialogue with traditional thought forms,* (John B. Taylor (ed.), Ibadan: Daystar Press, 1976). Archbishop Yannoulatos, speaking on 'Growing into an awareness of primal world-views', related his observations to the context of the forms of the Christian life that had grown in Africa as a result of the modern missionary movement from the West, noting the specific nature of Africa's pre-Christian religious heritage. He asked:

Have we offered the people of primal world-views the best we have? Have we made available to them all of the twenty-century-old tradition of the Church, not least that of the first centuries when Christians lived in a comparable climate of primal world-views? Or have missionaries only tried to transplant the Christianity and the problems of the western Europe of the 16th century onwards? Can it be true that, owing to these inadequacies, Christians from primal societies, as in Africa, were ...forced to seek to rediscover in their traditional rites some vital elements of the religious experience—such as the sense of total devotion, of being cut to the heart, of deep symbolism, or of participation of the whole person in worship? (Yannoulatos, 1976: 75-76).

For many years I have regarded ancient Greek religion and ancient Roman religion, that is, the religious background of the New Testament, as variants of primal religion, (in other words, of a similar nature to African traditional religion), even though, unlike the majority of modern primal religions, they had literary forms for their expression. The comments of Prof. Yannoulatos confirmed my own observations.

The third way to my conviction, accordingly, has to do with the new understanding of the primal religions of the world in the history and phenomenology of religion. These religions, like African traditional religions, and others in other parts of the world that share similar features, are called, in current religious scholarship, 'Primal Religions', because in the history and phenomenology of religion, they are generally recognised to be the religious traditions which enshrine the basal forms of human religious experience, as well as manifesting fundamental elements in the religious perception of life, and therefore constitute unique contributors to all other religions. In the entire twenty centuries of Christianity, it is mostly persons from these religious backgrounds who have found their spiritual home in the Christian faith.

The essential argument was made by Harold Turner in an article entitled, 'The primal religions of the world and their study' (Turner, 1977). Arguing for the educational importance of primal religions in religious studies within the Christian tradition, Turner drew attention to a 'special relationship' that primal religions have with Christianity, which arises from the fact that 'in the history of the spread of the Christian faith, its major extensions have been solely into the societies with primal religious systems'. This meant that 'the form of religion that might seem farthest removed from the Christian [from the standpoint of 19th and early 20th century Western missionary estimations of 'non-Christian religions'] has, in fact, had a closer relationship with it than any other.' Therefore it came as no surprise that 'it is the people of the primal religions who have made the greatest response' to the Christian faith.

There seem to be affinities between the Christian and the primal traditions, an affinity that perhaps appears in the common reactions when Christian missions first arrive ('this is what we have been waiting for') and that is further evident in the vast range of new religious movements born from the interaction between the primal religions and Christianity and in no comparable degree in the reaction of primal religions to their meeting with the other universal religions.

My point is twofold: we cannot avoid a serious engagement with the religious and spiritual issues that African Traditional Religions raise for us since they form the cultural background of the Christian faith of most African Christians. Also, the necessities of theological apologetics require that we make sense of our Christian affirmations only in relation to whatever alternatives are found in the contexts in which we make those affirmations.

In the rest of this article, I concern myself with the evangelical affirmation of the uniqueness of Jesus Christ in the religiously plural environment in which most of us live, a subject which, from the perspective of my evangelical self-understanding and from the standpoint of my African experience of reality, is important, whatever the particular nature of our Christian ministry.

Christ, unique in relation to 'other lords'

'Jesus is the Son of God', said the Christian evangelist.
'My shrine-spirit is also a child of God', said the traditionalist.
What is the next line in the discussion?

That sequence in a constructed conversation between a Christian preacher and an African religious traditionalist may be taken to illustrate the kind of issues that are at stake in the Christian affirmation of the uniqueness of Christ in the midst of the plurality of religions. It is not often recognised in Christian circles that theological affirmations about Christ are meaningful ultimately, not in terms of what Christians say, but in terms of what persons of other faiths understand those affirmations to imply for them. In other words, our Christian affirmations about the uniqueness of Christ achieve their real impact when they are subjected to the test to establish their credentials and validity not only in terms of the religious and spiritual universe in which Christians habitually operate, but also and indeed especially, in terms of the religious and spiritual worlds which persons of other faiths inhabit. For it is, after all, in those 'other worlds' that the true meaning of the unique Christ is meant to become apparent and validated.

Perhaps I need to stress that this procedure does not mean that Christian affirmations are to be shaped or determined by the content of other religious faiths, let alone be derived from those sources. The point is rather that by their very nature, Christian affirmations about the uniqueness of Christ arise from their relationship to the claims and presuppositions that are made by persons of other faiths for theirs. Essentially, there are no real grounds for affirming the uniqueness of Christ where there are no alternatives to be taken seriously. This is the understanding of the apostle Paul in 1 Corinthians 8:5-6, where his very affirmation that there is only one Lord, Jesus Christ, is made in relation to the other 'so-called many lords'. In other words, affirmation of uniqueness has meaning as it relates to alternative claims. Accordingly, the affirmation about the unique Lord Jesus Christ arises from how he is perceived in his relation to other 'lords'.

Christian affirmations - as recognition, not assertion

Once the affirmation about the unique Christ is expressed in the terms I have suggested, it may seem to be so self-evident that it might not need to be stated. And yet, in point of fact, it is because the nature of our Christian affirmations is so often misconstrued by Christians and non-Christians alike, that the issue can bear some elaboration.

It is perhaps not an exaggeration to say that there is a general tendency in Christian circles to treat Christian affirmations as essentially theological *data*, as some sort of fixed grid of doctrinal positions which have an inherent meaning in and of themselves, irrespective of their validation in terms other than those in which they are stated. The affirmation about the unique Christ, accordingly, becomes one such theological *datum*. While there may be a case for treating our own formulations of our doctrinal positions, our 'statements of faith', in this way, I am certain that we cannot do this with biblical affirmations. While biblical affirmations have the character of convictions, they are not given as fixed *data*. Rather, being an integral part of the total biblical revelation, they share in the character and purpose of that revelation. That is, they are given to provide the conditions for humans to make an identical response of faith in Jesus Christ who is revealed in the Scriptures, and to whom those affirmations bear witness. Within the Scriptures this process can be identified in the apostle Paul's statement in 2 Corinthians 4:13-14.

The truth of biblical revelation, therefore, is not just truth to be 'believed in' as by mere intellectual or mental assent; it is truth to be 'participated in'. By his faith in Christ, Paul finds that he has become a participant in the same truth as motivated the psalmist in Psalm 116:10. Another way of expressing this view is to say that the truth of biblical revelation is the truth, *not of assertion, but of recognition*. In that sense, a biblical affirmation concerning the uniqueness of Christ is not an arbitrary claim or assertion, made *a priori* in the interests of, or for the benefit of, any particular community, not even the Christian community. The affirmation is the fruit of recognition, and thus is intended to find its true significance in its application to the totality of humankind.

In reverse order, the affirmation provides the opportunity and the conditions for others to perceive or recognise its significance for them. It is in this way that it becomes possible to describe the entire biblical revelation as a witness, in other words, a witness that is borne by God, and especially to Jesus Christ, but also borne by those who, in response to the divine initiative, become partakers, by their recognition, in the truth of the divine witness. The cumulative effect of biblical revelation, understood as witness, is the expectation that it will generate similar recognition, by others, of the truth to which it bears witness, as in the well-known words of 1 John 1:1ff. The whole nature of the biblical revelation may be said to be summarised in these verses. They show that the climax of divine self-disclosure was not in a set of documented religious formulae or theological propositions, but rather in a life—in a human life which could be seen, looked upon and touched. And yet the quality of that human life was such that it provided, and continues to provide, clues for its recognition as truly divine in its origin, as it was truly human in its manifestation. Upon this recognition, Christian affirmation makes its claim that the human-divine life to which it bears witness is the light of the world and the life and hope of the whole of humankind.

To further clarify my argument, perhaps in counterpoint to another major religious faith, Islam, I may quote an observation by Andrew Walls:

> ... the true Christian analogy with the Qur'an is not the Bible but Christ. Christ for Christians, the Qur'an for Muslims, is the Eternal Word of God; but Christ is Word Translated. That fact is the sign that the contingent Scriptures (also describable as Word of God), unlike the Qur'an, may and should constantly be translated. .... Incarnation is translation. When God in Christ became man, Divinity was translated into humanity, as though humanity were a receptor language. Here was a clear statement of what would otherwise be veiled in obscurity or uncertainty, the statement, 'This is what God is like'. (Walls,1990:24f)

Essentially, then, the principle of recognition, focusing as it does on seeing Christ as God incarnate and accessible, becomes of crucial importance for rightly understanding the true character of the Christian affirmation concerning the uniqueness of Jesus Christ. This is what Jesus meant in John 5:39f.

The unique Christ (1): Religions as traditions of response

Once the point is granted that Christian affirmations about the uniqueness of Jesus Christ are not assertions, but rather invitations to recognition, it becomes essential to engage the major question: What then is it that in Christ confronts us, which calls for our recognition? This is the fundamental question regarding the status of the unique Christ amid the plurality of religions. It is to be

answered not by Christian claims alone, but also by conclusions arrived at
through working with the inward meanings of the religious worlds of other
faiths. This is so because the indication of the unique status of Jesus Christ is
seen, ultimately, in a demonstration that he is able to inhabit those other
worlds also as the Lord.

But even before we get to answer that fundamental question, there is a
preliminary matter to settle. Our starting-point can only be the ministry of
Jesus on earth, 'in the days of his flesh' (Hebrews 5:7, RSV), in other words,
as the divine self-disclosure in and through him was offered for recognition
to men and women. In this regard, it is, perhaps, instructive that in Paul's
summary of the Gospel in I Corinthians 15:3-9, he focuses on the actual
events of the life and ministry of Jesus. The point is that all these 'earthly'
events in the career of Jesus came to be recognised as signposts pointing the
way to what our salvation required. Paul's own personal testimony in vv. 9-
11 to the efficacy of these events for salvation, is the sign that these events,
validated by the witness of the Scriptures, did and do contain and offer the
conditions which make the recognition of their significance possible for
others too.

This concentration on the 'earthly' ministry of Jesus is valid, and indeed
necessary, because it is in the circumstances of our human earthly existence
that we are given to discern and to understand the religious dimension of
human life in the experiences of men and women. In turn, the religious
dimension in people's experiences becomes important as the focal point of
the encounter between our Christian affirmations, on the one hand, and the
plurality of the so-called 'non-Christian' religions, on the other–the religions
that provide the immediate universe of spiritual meanings for a large portion
of our fellow humans. This is another way of saying that it would be false to
conceive of the meeting of Christian affirmations with the religious meanings of other faiths in terms of mutually exclusive systems, or even of credal
formulations. Rather, the encounter takes place in the things that pertain to
the Spirit who, like the wind, blows where he wills. To quote Kenneth Cragg:

> In the mystery and the burden of the plurality of religions, there lies, surely,
> the supreme test of the meaning we intend when we say, 'I believe in the
> Holy Spirit'. (Cragg, 1968:71)

There is an obvious analogy here with the attempts found in some authors
in early Christian theology, particularly Justin Martyr and Clement of Alexandria, (see Bediako, 1992). The major difference between their approach and
my present approach is that in place of their use of the notion of the pre-
Incarnate Word (Logos) who operated as much in extra-biblical tradition as
in the biblical, I evoke the activity of the Holy Spirit.

Since we are concerned with religions, not as 'belief-systems', but as the
matrix in which men and women experience and respond to the sacred in

their human existence, it is possible to agree with John V. Taylor on how we may regard other peoples' faiths:

> I believe it is truer to think of a religion as a people's tradition of response to the reality the Holy Spirit has set before their eyes. I am deliberately not saying that any religion is the truth which the Spirit disclosed, nor even that it contains that truth. All we can say without presumption is that this is how men have responded and taught others to respond to what the Spirit made them aware of. It is the history of a particular answer, a series of answers, to the call and claim of him who lies beyond all religions. (Taylor, 1972:182)

Looked at as 'a tradition of response' to the reality and disclosure of the Transcendent, every religion can be probed, therefore, not so much for the measure of truth it contains, as for the truth of the human response to the divine action within that tradition. As a tradition of response, every religion also displays within it, 'the same tension between conservatism and development which characterises all human response to the call of God which comes through the new situation' (Taylor, 1972:183). In other words, within every religion, there are indicators which point *towards* Christ, and there are indicators which point *away* from Christ. However, our concern is not so much with those indicators themselves, as with the *human* responses that are made to those indicators.

It becomes possible, then, also to speak of a plurality within every religious tradition. Thus, it is possible to understand how one response to Old Testament religious teaching can lead to the Mishnah and the Talmud, and the rejection of the messiahship of our Lord Jesus Christ, whilst another response can lead to the New Testament and the recognition of the same Jesus Christ as Lord, Messiah and Saviour of the whole world.

The unique Christ (2): What is it that, in Christ, confronts us?

Granted that the Christian affirmation about the unique status of our Lord Jesus Christ in the midst of the plurality of religions encounters traditions of response to the disclosure of the Transcendent that the Holy Spirit sets before people, our task in Christian apologetics is to demonstrate how the Scriptural witness to the life and ministry of Jesus Christ, illuminated by the Holy Spirit, is the clue to the yearnings and quests in the religious lives of people. As Bishop Kenneth Cragg remarks, 'the critical question for the Christian' is 'how to have the meanings of Christ become operative in human hearts' (Cragg, 1977:116). Here, there are three aspects of Christian affirmation about Christ which readily stand out for consideration. The first is the affirmation concerning the Incarnation, namely, the affirmation that in Christ,

God humbled himself and identified with humankind in Christ's birth as a human baby, born of woman, and endured the conditions of 'normal' human existence—in other words, the Incarnation is supremely the unique sign and demonstration of divine vulnerability in history.

The second aspect relates to the Christian affirmation about the Cross of Christ, showing that the will to suffer forgivingly and redemptively is the very expression of the divine mind and the logic of the divine love. Accordingly all other attempts to achieve redemptive ends apart from the way of the Cross, are shown to be partial and inadequate.

The third aspect relates to the communion at the Lord's Table, in which the invitation to all who are united to Christ in faith to partake of the holy emblems of bread and wine—symbols of Jesus Christ's redemptive achievement through his body and blood—demonstrates the uniqueness of the making of one people out of the many of humankind. Accordingly, the reconciliation of broken relationships across racial, ethnic, national, cultural, social and economic barriers becomes an important test of the authenticity of a people's response to the disclosure of the Transcendent which the Holy Spirit sets before them.

It is possible to reformulate these three aspects of what confronts us in the ministry of Jesus Christ as follows: in Jesus Christ, the Holy Spirit reveals to us a divine paradigm which confronts all religions, challenging men and women in three specific areas—in our understanding of power and weakness, in our response to evil, and in our response to cultural and social enmity and exclusiveness. It is by these down-to earth clues to the divine paradigm disclosed in the ministry of Jesus Christ that all religions are challenged and invited to make an equally concrete response, in faith, repentance and obedience. In this respect, Christianity too, in all its different traditions and denominations, being formally equivalent to the other religions as traditions of response, is challenged to respond to the unique Christ who is the Lord. For,

It is not Christianity that saves, but Christ. (Walls, 1996:66)

In Jesus Christ, then, we have the threefold paradigm of divine vulnerability, the will to redemptive suffering and reconciling love, not as abstract notions, but as concrete events and deeds in a human life, and achieved in ways which Christian faith reads as expressive of the divine nature itself. As the Gospel of Mark records of yet another instance of recognition:

When the centurion, who stood facing him, saw that he thus breathed his last, he said, 'Truly, this man was the Son of God'. (Mark 15:39, RSV)

What, therefore, in Jesus Christ, confront us, are clues that point us to the recognition of divine self-disclosure and guide us to the consequent challenge to discipleship to the One in whose incarnate life that disclosure has been given. Thus the Christian affirmation about the unique status of Jesus Christ in the midst of the plurality of religions does not arise, first and foremost, from theological propositions or credal formulations, or from our statements of faith. It arises from the recognition of the divine nature expressed in actual historical existence. Bishop Kenneth Cragg is right to point out:

> [Our Lord's] Sonship, then, before it becomes a term in creeds, is a reality in deeds. ... Sonship in that immediate, existential sense, was the context of his doing. Therefore we take it also as the secret of his being. If Jesus is 'Son of God' in the music of the *Te Deum* and in the confessions of Nicea and Chalcedon, it is because he was the Son of God beneath the olive branches of Gethsemane and in the darkness of Golgotha. (Cragg, 1977:56)

What remains important is to realise that the focus of the Christian affirmation is not the assertion of a formula, but the recognition of an achievement in actual history which, in turn, provides clues to the source of those deeds. Hebrews 5:8-10 expresses the same thought.

The consistent New Testament pattern of affirmation about Jesus Christ, therefore, is to work *from* the actual historical achievement in the life, ministry, death and resurrection of Jesus Christ, *to* the theological elaboration of the universal significance and application of that achievement.

If we wish to follow the pattern and approach of the New Testament in our affirmation of the unique status of Jesus Christ in the midst of the plurality of religions of our modern context, then we too can have what Bishop Cragg calls a 'sober, critical confidence' (Cragg, 1977:59) that the actual history of the achievement in the ministry of Jesus Christ is able to stake its claims in the religious worlds of other faiths. In other words, the meanings of Christ as given in the symbols of the Incarnation, the Cross and the reconciling fellowship at the Lord's Table, can become operative in human hearts because he belongs there, and because whatever is ultimate in the religious universe of every 'tradition of response', at least in intention, is Christ.

Christian apologetics and the possibility of new theological idioms

If this view is granted, then it is also another way of saying that the encounter between Christ and the meanings inherent in other religions takes place in the terms of those meanings themselves. Acts 14:15-17 and Acts 17:22-34 indicate that this is a possibility. In the passage in question, the apostles suggest to their hearers that even though in the past their prayers have been made to their own gods, in so far as their requests have been expressions of legitimate needs, it is the God and Father of our Lord Jesus Christ who has answered them and provided those needs!

In the light of such an understanding, it also becomes possible, in our

Christian apologetics, to explore new theological idioms without surrender-
ing Christian content, for Christian content, strictly, is Jesus Christ himself.
In the previous chapter, I explored some of the new meanings of Jesus Christ
within a Ghanaian cultural context, demonstrating that, in relation to the spiritual universe of African primal religions, for instance, it is possible to apply
to Jesus Christ the religiously significant category of Ancestor, but in a far
richer sense than is traditionally held about lineage ancestors.

Conclusion: Christian apologetics amid other religious faiths—the continuing encounter

Conceivably, it may be objected that the approach I propose is too open-
ended, and, perhaps, even risky, for I leave many questions unresolved from
the start, and I hold many Christian theological propositions and credal
formulations in abeyance. My response would be that such an approach,
precisely, through openness and vulnerability, is what Christian witness to
the divine incognito in Christ requires.

The important question is: Does our affirmation of the unique status of
our Lord Jesus Christ have to require that we coerce belief in him by discred-
iting the religious values of other faiths as 'traditions of response to the reality of the Transcendent'? If, on the other hand, the uniqueness of Jesus Christ
consists, not in how far apart he stands from us, but rather in how accessible
he is to all of us, then it seems that we can also say that our proclamation
and affirmation of the uniqueness of Jesus Christ in the midst of other faiths,
consists in commending the meanings of Jesus Christ as disclosed to us in
the Scriptures, to men and women in their own worlds of faith, respecting
their personality as beings created, like ourselves, in the image of the one
and the same Creator, and yet seeking to 'move them Christward in the freedom of their personal wills' (Cragg, 1977:166). Accordingly, the practice of
evangelical Christian apologetics becomes also an exercise in spirituality,
one in which we affirm a commitment to the ultimacy of Jesus Christ, whilst
accepting the integrity of other faiths and those who profess them.

I wish finally to refer to another massive 'other faith' operating in our
context, Islam. I do so by recalling a remark by John Taylor, citing Kenneth
Cragg, on what lies at the heart of Christian-Muslim differences. The observation helps to focus our attention again on the encounter which truly takes
place 'in the things that pertain to the Spirit', as expressed in actual history:

> The contradictions between Muslim and Christian fidelity can be seen to
> arise in large part from the different ways in which the Messiah and the
> Prophet responded to the same situation when it confronted them. Each
> was sure of his call to show men a new way, preaching, gathering the
> crowds, training his disciples; and each was faced with the opposition of

the religious leaders, rejection and disaffection of his followers. What did he do? Jesus chose to go on in the same way, in the same spirit. He bowed his head to what was coming; he accepted rejection, failure and death, entrusting the outcome to God. In the case of Mohammed, it looked for a moment as if he too would take the way of suffering; but then he decided to fight back on behalf of the truth. He raised his army and marched on Mecca, and that was the turning point in his career and the birth of Islam. From these two choices, one can derive the fundamental difference between Christian and Muslim ideas of God's nature. The gulf between them is seen, as it were, in cross section; for it is nothing less than the cross which is now demanding our decision. Once more we see that the evangelism of the Holy Spirit consists in creating the occasion for choice. The servant of the Gospel can do no less and perhaps need do no more. (Taylor, 1972:188-89)

Bishop Taylor's observations bring us full circle: Authentic Christian apologetics also implies providing, in Christ-like humility and in Christ-like vulnerability, the conditions that make it possible for others to perceive and recognise Jesus as Christ the Lord.

References

Bediako, K., 1990: *Jesus in African Culture—a Ghanaian perspective*, (Accra: Asempa Publishers).
– 1992: *Theology and Identity—the impact of culture upon Christian thought in the second century and modern Africa*, (Oxford: Regnum Books; reprinted 1999).
Cragg, Kenneth, 1968: *Christianity in World Perspective*, (London: Lutterworth Press).
– 1977: *The Christian and other religion—the Measure of Christ*, (London & Oxford: Mowbrays).
Taylor, John V., 1972: *The Go-Between God—The Holy Spirit and the Christian Mission*, (London: SCM Press).
Turner, H.W., 1977: 'The primal religions of the world and their study', in Victor Hayes (ed.) *Australian Essays in World Religions*, (Bedford Park: Australian Association for World Religions), 27-37.
Walls, Andrew F., 1990: 'The translation principle in Christian history', in P.C. Stine (ed.), *Bible translation and the spread of the Church—the last 200 years*, (Leiden: E.J. Brill), 24-39. [Also in *The Missionary Movement in Christian History, Studies in the Transmission of Faith*, (Edinburgh/New York: T. & T. Clark/Orbis Books), 26-42.]
– 1996, 'Romans One and the modern missionary movement', in *The Missionary Movement in Christian History*, 55-67.
Yannoulatos, Anastasios, 1976: 'Growing into awareness of primal world-views', in John B. Taylor (ed.), *Primal World-Views: Christian involvement in dialogue with traditional thought forms*, (Ibadan: Daystar Press), 72-78.

II. Theology and Culture

CHAPTER 4

Understanding African theology in the twentieth century

African Christian thought in the post-missionary era: Liberation and integration

It is now well-known that two distinct trends emerged in African Christian thought in the post-independence and post-missionary era, from the late 1950s to the late 1980s. The one was the theological dimension to the struggle for the social and political transformation of the conditions of inequality and oppression in South Africa. This produced Black theology, a theology of liberation in the African setting and in response to the particular circumstances of southern Africa. The other was the theological exploration into the indigenous cultures of African peoples, with particular stress on their pre-Christian (and also pre-Islamic) religious traditions. This trend was more closely associated with the rest of tropical Africa, where political independence took away a direct experience of the socio-political pressures that produced Black theology in South Africa. Here the broad aim was to achieve integration between the African pre-Christian religious experience and African Christian commitment in ways that would ensure the integrity of African Christian identity and selfhood.

Although this article focuses on the second of these 'trends', generally designated 'African theology', the two are by no means to be regarded as mutually exclusive, but may be seen as 'a series of concentric circles of which Black theology is the inner and smaller circle' (Tutu, 1987:54).

An early shared concern: The African religious past as a prime theological issue

The predominant concern with the pre-Christian religious traditions of Africa in the early literature of African theology has been characterised sometimes as an unhealthy, inward-looking preoccupation with an imagined African past. No less an interpreter of African Christianity than Adrian Hastings has made this criticism (Hastings, 1989:30-35). At the same time, African non-Christian critics have vehemently rejected what they have regarded as African theology's attempt to 'christianise', and hence to distort, African tradition. For them, the effort to seek an integration of the pre-Christian religious tradition and African Christian experience is misplaced and unwarranted, being the search for the reconciliation of essentially and intrinsically antithetical entities (p'Bitek, 1970; Mazrui, 1980).

However, it is significant that it is a practitioner of Black theology who has made one of the most positive evaluations of African theology and of its achievements:

> African theologians have set about demonstrating that the African religious experience and heritage were not illusory, and that they should have formed the vehicle for conveying the Gospel verities to Africa... It was vital for the African's self-respect that this kind of rehabilitation of his religious heritage should take place... It has helped to give the lie to the supercilious but tacit assumption that religion and history in Africa date from the advent in that continent of the white man. It is reassuring to know that we have had a genuine knowledge of God and that we have had our own ways of communicating with deity, ways which meant that we were able to speak authentically as ourselves and not as pale imitators of others. It means that we have a great store from which we can fashion new ways of speaking to and about God, and new styles of worship consistent with our new faith. (Tutu, 1978: 366)

Archbishop Tutu's observations are a strong affirmation that the effort made in African theology to 'rehabilitate Africa's rich cultural heritage and religious consciousness' has been valid, but it remains important to appreciate why this effort was made as a self-consciously *theological* endeavour, and in a specifically *Christian* interest. Writing on early developments in African theology in *African Christianity—An essay in interpretation,* Adrian Hastings drew attention to the fact that 'the chief non-Biblical reality with which the African theologian must struggle is the non-Christian religious tradition of his own people', and that African theology early became 'something of a dialogue between the African scholar and the perennial religions and spiritualities of Africa' (Hastings, 1976:50f). For Hastings, this was frustrating, for it meant that 'areas of traditional Christian doctrine which are not reflected in the African past disappear or are marginalised'. He was particularly concerned about the absence of serious discussion on Christology.

It is not hard to see what had happened: the same religious traditions—the primal religions of Africa—that were generally deemed unworthy of serious theological consideration in missionary times, now occupied 'the very centre of the academic stage' (Hastings, 1976:183), in African theological reflection. In the light of the conclusion at the Edinburgh 1910 World Missionary Conference that Africa's primal religions 'contained no preparation for Christianity' (*The Missionary Message,* 1910:24), it becomes crucial to understand this heightened theological interest in the primal religions of Africa if we are to interpret correctly the pioneer writers of African theology, to duly recognise their achievement, and to discern accurately the trends and directions they set.

African theology and the shaping of a method—theology as the hermeneutic of identity

To the extent that African theology's effort at 'rehabilitating Africa's cultural heritage and religious consciousness' has been pursued as self-consciously *Christian* and *theological,* it may be said to have been an endeavour at demonstrating the true character of African *Christian* identity. For, from the standpoint of the context of the writers themselves, the primal religions of Africa belong to the African religious past. Yet this is not so much a chronological past as an 'ontological' past. The theological importance of such an ontological past consists in the fact that it belongs together with the profession of the Christian faith in giving account of the same entity, namely, the history of the religious consciousness of the African Christian. In this sense the theological concern with the African pre-Christian religious heritage becomes an effort to clarify the nature and meaning of African Christian identity and a quest for what Kenneth Cragg describes as 'integrity in conversion, a unity of self in which one's past is genuinely integrated into present commitment, so that the crisis of repentance and faith that makes us Christian truly integrates what we have been in what we become' (Cragg, 1980:194). It is the same notion that E.W. Fasholé-Luke had in mind in his statement that 'the quest for African Christian theologies... amounts to attempting to make clear the fact that conversion to Christianity must be coupled with cultural continuity' (Fasholé-Luke, 1975:267).

From the perspective of African Christian identity, the missionary presumption of European value-setting for the Christian faith, that led to the exclusion of any 'preparation for Christianity' in African primal religions, could only produce the *problematik* John Mbiti described when he wrote of the post-missionary Church in Africa as a 'Church without theology and without theological consciousness' (Mbiti, 172:51). This was the result of not allowing for the existence of a pre-Christian memory in African Christian consciousness. For theological consciousness presupposes religious tradition, and tradition requires memory, and memory is integral to identity: without memory we have no past, and if we have no past, we lose our identity. Andrew F. Walls, commenting on the literature of African theology, rightly identified the heart of the theological investigation of the religious past:

No question is more clamant than the African Christian identity crisis. It is not simply an intellectual quest. The massive shift in the centre of gravity of

the Christian world which has taken place cannot be separated from the
cultural impact of the West in imperial days. Now the Empires are dead
and the Western value-setting of the Christian faith largely rejected. Where
does this leave the African Christian? Who is he? What is his past? A past
is vital for all of us—without it, like the amnesiac man, we cannot know
who we are. The prime African theological quest at present is this: what is
the past of the African Christian? What is the relationship between Africa's
old religions and her new one? (Walls, 1978:12)

It is not surprising, therefore, that 'the central theme of this literature'
became 'the nature of the traditional religion of Africa and its relationship
of continuity rather than discontinuity with Christian belief' (Hastings, 1976:
50). This theme of continuity would be pursued with varying degrees of
vigour by different writers, but it became a common concern because of
some equally common factors that in turn helped to shape African theology.
These included: the need to respond to the sense of a theological *problematik*
in African Christianity produced by the widespread perception that the Western value-setting for the Christian faith in the missionary era had entailed a
far-reaching underestimation of the African knowledge and sense of God;
the unavoidable element of Africa's continuing primal religions, not as the
remnants of an outworn 'primitive mentality', but in terms of their world-
view, as living realities in the experience of vast numbers of African Christians in all the churches, and not only in the so-called Independent Churches;
and the intellectual struggle for, and 'feeling after', a theological method in a
field of enquiry that had hitherto been charted largely by Western anthropological scholarship in terminology relating to Africa that would often be
'unacceptable' to Africans. Terms like 'fetish', 'animist', 'polytheistic',
'primitive', 'uncivilised' and 'lower'—the Western intellectual categories
devised to describe and interpret African religious tradition. Each of these,
African theology would reject. It is significant how virtually all the pioneer
writers of this formative period of African theology, though trained in theology on Western models, in their academic and intellectual careers in Africa
became engaged in areas of study and writing for which no Western theological syllabus had prepared them, being 'forced to study and lecture on
African Traditional Religion, ... and each one writing on it' (Walls, 1996:13).
    It is remarkable that the practitioners of African theology took on the chal-
lenge of re-interpreting African primal religions, approaching the subject,
'not as historians of religion do, nor as anthropologists do, but as Christian
theologians' (Walls, 1996:13), and arriving at some startling conclusions.
When African theologians describe African Primal religions in terms of
'monotheism' or 'diffused monotheism', as Bolaji Idowu did with regard to
Yoruba religion (Idowu, 1962:62; 1973:168); or when John Mbiti, reversing
the verdict of the Edinburgh World Missionary Conference, called African
pre-missionary religious experience a *praeparatio evangelica,* (Mbiti,

1970:36), they are to be understood as drawing on their sense of belonging within Christian tradition and using categories that describe their understanding of *their* pre-Christian heritage, related to *their* Christian commitment.

The failure in some criticisms of African theology may be traced to a misconception about what the tasks of these African Christian writers ought to be. When John Mbiti's *Concepts of God in Africa* is objected to for its 'primary theological purpose', as 'attempting to lay the basis for a distinctively African theology by blending the African past with the Judeo-Christian tradition' (Ray, 1976:15); or when his *The Prayers of African Religion* is judged to be 'unsatisfactory' because 'it tends to blur the distinctiveness of African spirituality by seeking a *praeparatio evangelica* rather than the integrity of the cult-group' (McKenzie, 1975-76:220-21), such criticisms obscure the contributions that these African theologians could be making towards the understanding of what is, after all, their own religious heritage; which is, indeed, a proper task of theology. In both these instances, the critics rightly interpret the intention of the African theologian. It just so happens that they do not approve of what they find. Yet, if an underlying motivation of the quest for an African Christian theology was an endeavour 'to draw together the various and disparate sources which make up the total religious experience of Christians in Africa into a coherent and meaningful pattern' (Fasholé-Luke, 1975:268), then African theology is more accurately judged by its own 'primary theological purpose' than by any extraneous criteria.

Once it is granted that African theology's investigations into African primal religions are qualitatively different from the observations of anthropologists, it becomes possible to appreciate how, by its fundamental motivation, African theology may have been charting a new course in theological method. It is not that this course has no parallel in the totality of Christian scholarship, for the categories were being derived from Christian tradition as much as from African experience and realm of ideas. Rather, this new theological approach had no counterpart in the more recent Western theological thought forged within the context of Christendom.

At the heart of the new theological method would be the issue of identity, which would itself be perceived as a theological category, and which therefore entailed confronting constantly the question as to how, and how far, the 'old' and the 'new' in African religious consciousness could become integrated into a unified vision of what it meant to be African *and* Christian. The issue of identity in turn forced the theologian to become the *locus* of this struggle for integration through a dialogue which, to be authentic, was bound to become personal and so infinitely more intense. The African Christian theologian is quite often 'handling dynamite, his own past, his people's present', a far cry from 'the clinical observations of the sort one might make about Babylonian religion' (Walls, 1996:13). Hence the development of theological concern and the formulation of theological questions became linked as the unavoidable by-product of this process of Christian self-definition.

A range of responses—Indigenisers, biblicists and translators

Against this background of a common concern, there emerged, nevertheless, divergences and differences, some of which were considerable. While
the theme of continuity was central, the terms in which the argument was
pursued differed among its protagonists. The pace-setter in the argument for
a radical continuity was Bolaji Idowu. Founded on the continuity and the
unity of God (Idowu, 1962; 1969), the argument was coupled with an equally
strong case made for a 'radical indigenisation of the Church' (Idowu, 1965),
on the grounds that the church in Africa, as a result of its peculiar historical
connection with Western cultural dominance, was failing to develop its own
theology, churchmanship, liturgy, or even discipline. In order to remedy this
'predicament' of dependence (Idowu, 1968), the African church needed to
build its bridges to the 'revelation' given to Africans in their pre-Christian
and pre-missionary religious traditions of the past (Idowu, 1965:26). Osten-
sibly intended to connect the 'old' and the 'new' in African religious experience, the fundamental postulate of the 'foreignness of Christianity' which
underlies this position, tended towards a minimalist reading of the newness
of Christianity in Africa at the specific level of religious apprehension. African
Christian experience emerged as not much more than a refinement of the
experience of the 'old' religion (Idowu, 1962:202; 1973:209). The vindication and the affirmation of African selfhood, which, at the start, had been
conceived as the task of the church, later came to be entrusted to the revital-
isation of the 'old' religions, with their 'God-given-heritage of indigenous
spiritual and cultural treasures' (Idowu, 1973: 205). This perspective found
an echo in later writers, such as Gabriel Setiloane (1976; 1978), Samuel Kibicho (1978) and Christian Gaba (1968; 1969; 1977).

A less radical example of the same concern with continuity was the work
of another 'pace-setter' and vindicator of the claims of a specifically African
religious consciousness especially among francophone and predominantly
Roman Catholic theologians, the Congolese scholar, Mulago, and the 'school'
of thought that grew from his researches at the *Centre d'Etudes des Religions
Africaines* in Kinshasa (Mulago, 1957). He retained a firm conviction regarding the relevance of the Christian message for Africa, but insisted that the
process of forging the new integration 'cannot be solid and viable except as
it remains faithful to ancestral traditions and as it manages to be judicious in
its contact with the civilisations of other peoples and with revealed religion'
(Mulago, 1980:7). In its more radical forms, this perspective, with its fundamental postulate of the *foreignness* of the Christianity transmitted in Africa,
as well as its minimalist view of the *newness* of the Christian faith in relation to African religious tradition, was always in danger of leading *Christ-*

ian reflection into an impasse. For if the Christian Gospel brought little that was new to Africa in religious terms, then in what lay the value and the rationale of the quest for a specifically *Christian* theological thought in Africa? The writings of Bolaji Idowu represent an acute form of this dilemma.

At the other end of the spectrum was the radical discontinuity stoutly championed by Byang Kato, representing the thought of those Christian churches and groups linked with the Association of Evangelicals of Africa (formerly 'of Africa and Madagascar'), who trace their spiritual heritage, in the main, to the missionary work of western faith missions in Africa. Basing himself on a radical Biblicism, Kato stressed the distinctiveness of the experience of the Christian Gospel to such an extent that he rejected the positive evaluation of any pre-Christian religious tradition as a distraction from the necessary 'emphasis on Bible truth' (Kato, 1975:169). Kato's insistence on the centrality of the Bible for the theological enterprise in Africa must be reckoned a most important contribution to African Christian thought. Yet his outright rejection of the understanding of theology as a synthesis of 'old' and 'new' in a quest for a unified framework for dealing with culturally-rooted questions, meant that Kato's perspective could not provide a sufficient foundation for the tradition of creative theological engagement that the African context seemed to be requiring. Before long, other evangelicals, without denying their commitment to the centrality of the Bible for the theological enterprise, were seeking more positive ways whereby the Christian Gospel might encounter African tradition (Tiénou, 1982).

However, the largest portion of the literature of African theology has been in the middle ground between the two radical positions. As well as a widespread consensus that there exists an African pre-Christian religious heritage to be taken seriously, there has been also the realisation that it is important to recognise the integrity of African *Christian* experience as a religious reality in its own right, and that Christianity as a religious faith is not intrinsically foreign to Africa. It has deep roots in the long histories of the peoples of the continent, whilst it has proved to be capable of apprehension by Africans in *African* terms, as is demonstrated by the massive and diverse presence of the faith in African life. The eternal Gospel has already found a local home within the African response to it, showing that Christ has become the integrating reality and power linking 'old' and 'new' in the African experience.

This perspective seemed to offer the most hopeful signs for the development of a sustainable tradition of an African Christian thought into the future, having firmly taken on board the critical notion that the Christian faith is capable of 'translation' into African terms without injury to its essential content. Consequently, the task of African theology, came to consist, not in 'indigenising' Christianity, or theology as such, but in letting the Christian Gospel encounter, as well as be shaped by, the African experience. This task could proceed without anxiety about its possibility, but also without apology to Western traditions of Christianity, since the Western traditions did not

enshrine universal norms. The overall goal of African theology was to show
that there were genuinely and specifically *African* contributions—derived
from the twin heritage of African Christianity, namely, the African primal
tradition and the African experience of the Christian Gospel—to be made to
the theology of the universal Church. Some of the best-known exemplars of
this perspective have been Harry Sawyerr (1968), John Mbiti (1970) and
Kwesi Dickson (1984).

The 1990s —Into new directions

It may be helpful to consider the decade of the 1980s as a period of transition, as earlier writers brought their major work to a close, (some, such as
Idowu, seemed to have begun to do so even in the 1970s), and a new generation was emerging to continue from where the earlier had left off. While the
broad concerns of the relationship of the primal religions to Christianity still
retained interest, all the indications were that a watershed had been passed.
The fortunes of African Christianity had ceased to be beholden to Western
assessments and interpretations of Africa. Not what Western missionaries did
or said (or failed to do or say), but what African Christians would do with
their Christian faith and commitment were now the determining factors in
the development of Christian thought in Africa (Appiah-Kubi, 1979).

An indication that the early concentration on the theological meaning of
the pre-Christian primal heritage had been appropriate was the fact that a
later generation of African theologians, in exploring other themes, could take
off from genuinely African categories. This was most markedly so in relation to christological discussion, which had been conspicuously minimal or
absent in earlier writings. It is interesting, however, that much of the 'new'
concern with christological explorations began around categories such as,
Christ as *Healer,* as *Master of Initiation* and as *Ancestor*—all derived directly
from the apprehension of reality and of the Transcendent as experienced
within the world-views of African primal religions (Pobee, 1979; Bediako,
1984; 1990; Sanon, 1982; Nyamiti, 1984; Bujo, 1992; Schreiter, 1991). Apart
from Christology, the 'new' African theology was also seriously engaging
with subjects such as African Christian theological discourse and methodology (Tschibangu, 1979; 1980), soteriology and conversion (Okorocha, 1987),
as well as the history of Christian expansion and diffusion (Sanneh, 1989)·
and historical theology, in which issues in contemporary African Christianity
were being related to the Christian tradition as a whole (Bediako, 1992). It
seemed as though the growing realisation that Africa, in the late 20th century,
had become one of the heartlands of the Christian faith itself, had substan-
tially registered in African scholarship. In 1983, in an innovative investigation of West African Christian history, Lamin Sanneh concluded:

No one can miss the vitality of the [Christian] religion in much of the continent ... African Christianity may well have entered upon a universal vocation in the onward march of the people of God in history, a destiny comparable to that of Gentile Christianity in the early Christian centuries. (Sanneh, 1983)

It is no mean achievement, then, that African theology, by the agenda it set for itself from the start, as well as by the method it evolved, managed to overturn virtually every negative verdict passed on African tradition by the ethnocentrism of the Western missionary enterprise. It is a mark of that achievement that African theology has succeeded in providing an *African* re-interpretation of African pre-Christian religious tradition in ways that have ensured that the pursuit of a creative, constructive and perhaps also a self-critical, theological enterprise in Africa is not only viable, but distinctly possible, as a variant of the universal and continuing encounter of the Christian faith with the realities of human societies and their histories.

African theology—A feeling after new languages?

The era of African theological literature as reaction to Western misrepresentation is past. What lies ahead is a critical theological construction that will relate more fully the widespread African confidence in the Christian faith to the actual and ongoing Christian responses to the life-experiences of Africans. Academic theological discourse will need to connect with the fundamental reality of the 'implicit' and predominantly *oral* theologies found at the grassroots of many African Christian communities, where, in the words of John Mbiti, 'much of the theological activity in Christian Africa today is being done as oral theology, from the living experiences of Christians ...theology in the open from the pulpit, in the market-place in the home as people pray or read and discuss the Scriptures' (Mbiti, 1986:229; also 1979) This process may validate Adrian Hastings' early observation that:

It is in vernacular prayer, both public and private, both formal and informal and in the spirituality which grows up from such experience that the true roots of an authentic African Christianity will most surely be found. (Hastings, 1976:49)

It may be suggested that it is in modern Africa that Christianity's essential character as an 'infinitely [culturally] translatable' faith (Walls, 1996:25) has been most notably demonstrated in recent Christian history. This recognition and its impact on missionary action had the effect of loosening the grip of any 'Western possessiveness' of the faith in the process of its transmission (Cragg, 1968:15-28). Whenever Western missionaries or a missionary society made the Scriptures available to an African people in that people's own language, they weakened any Western bias in their presentation of the Gospel. African Christians, with access to the Bible in their mother-tongues, could truly claim they were hearing God speak to them in their own language. It amounts to the awareness that *God speaks our language too.*

Indeed, the possession of the Christian Scriptures in African languages, which could probably be regarded as the single most important element of the Western missionary legacy in Africa (Bediako, 1985:303-11)—in some cases, the Scriptures becoming the foundation for a new literary culture that did not exist previously (Sanneh, 1989)—ensured that an effectual rooting of the Christian faith took place in African consciousness. This ensured also a deep and authentic dialogue between the Gospel and African tradition, authentic in so far as it would take place, not in the terms of a foreign language or of an alien culture, but in the categories of local languages, idioms and world-views. At this point, one may ask why African Christian theologians have not followed the logic of the translatability of their faith into a full-blown recourse to African indigenous languages (Bediako, 1989:65). Perhaps it was to this problem that the late Cameroonian theologian, Engelbert Mveng attempted to respond, though somewhat polemically:

> When the objection is made that this theology is not written in native languages, we reply that it is *lived* in native languages, in the villages and in the neighbourhoods, before being translated into foreign languages by its own rightful heirs, the African theologians. (Mveng, 1988:18)

Mveng's comment points to the impact that a 'translatable faith', apprehended through mother-tongues, has had in Africa. The emergence of a significant African theological tradition in the 20th century, even if articulated predominantly in 'foreign languages', indicates that in African Christian life there is a substratum of vital Christian consciousness and a sufficiently deep apprehension of Jesus Christ at the level of religious experience, itself of a theological nature, that is the basis for a viable academic and literary theology. The translated Bible has provided an essential ingredient for the 'birth of theology' (Allmen, 1975:37-52). The fact remains that the seriousness with which African theology treats African mother-tongues as a fundamental medium in its theological discourse, may be an important test of the depth of the impact of the Bible and of the Christian faith itself in African life and determine the directions in which African theology too will grow.

African theology—A relevance beyond Africa?

Since African theology developed also as an African response to Western views and interpretations of African pre-Christian traditions, it may be worth exploring whether the African Christian thought that has emerged has relevance for the same process beyond Africa. In relation to our present discussion, what is important is the fact that Europe shares with Africa a pre-Christian primal religious heritage. But it is in Africa (as in other parts of the non-Western world) that the significance of the primal religions in the history of Christianity has been seen for what it is. In the case of Europe, Christian mission on the basis of substitution appears to have been pursued to such an extent that the primal traditions were virtually completely wiped out.

What this, together with the fact that there was no sustained interest in the use of indigenous European languages and their pre-Christian world-views for Christian purposes, has done to the Western religious memory may never be fully recovered.The European story suggests that the primal religions of Europe quickly became a spent force. Yet Christians continued to name the days of the week after pre-Christian deities, and pre-Christian elements and notions made their way into the celebration of Christian festivals, indicating that the old beliefs had not entirely lost their hold upon people's minds. It may be that in Africa the opportunity lost in Europe for a serious and creative theological encounter between the Christian and primal traditions, can be regained. The fact that African theology at its formative stage in the immediate post-missionary era focused on the theological interpretation of the African pre-Christian religious heritage may signify that such an encounter is possible; and it could be argued that in the process, African theology gains rather than loses. For, having been forced to do theology in the interface of their Christian faith and the perennial spiritualities of their African primal heritage, and having to internalise that dialogue within themselves, African theologians have restored the character of theology as Christian intellectual activity on the frontier with the non-Christian world, as essentially *communicative, evangelistic* and *missionary* (Verkuyl, 1978:277).

Even more significant has been the underlying argument that space had to be made for a positive pre-Christian religious memory in the African Christian consciousness, on the basis that 'religion informs the African's life in its totality' (Dickson, 1984:29), and that memory is integral to identity. To the extent that the African endeavour has been successful, it holds promise for a modern Western theology now asking how Christian faith may be related, in a *missionary* sense, to Western culture (Newbigin, 1986; 1987; 1989; 1991). For the African vindication of the theological significance of African primal religions may indicate that the European primal heritage was not illusory, to be consigned to oblivion as primitive darkness. A serious Christian theological interest in the European primal traditions and in the early forms of Christianity that emerged from the encounter with those traditions, could provide a fresh approach to understanding Christian identity in the West, as well as opening new possibilities for Christian theological endeavour today. The primal world view may turn out to be not so alien to the West after all, even in a post-Enlightenment era.

For aspects of the *post-modernist* rejection of the Enlightenment in the West—the resurgence of the phenomenon of the occult as well as the various 'quests' for spiritual experience and wholeness, even if without explicit reference to God—bear the marks of a primal world-view. They are sufficient indicators that a primal world-view, suppressed rather than encountered, redeemed and integrated, rises to haunt the future. The viability of Christian consciousness that retains its sense of the spiritual world of primal religions, and the theological encounter between the primal world view and Christian faith evident in African Christianity—constitute an implicit challenge to the notion that humanity can be fully defined in post-Enlightenment terms.

Primal religions, in Europe as in Africa and elsewhere, the religious traditions most closely associated historically with the continuing Christian presence in the world, may again point the way into the Christian future and the future of Christian theology (Walls, 1996:143-59). If this expectation proves right, the African contribution will have been an important one.

References

Allmen, Daniel von, 1975: ''The birth of theology—Contextualisation as the dynamic element in the formation of New Testament theology', in *International Review of Mission*, vol. 64, January,(1975), 37-52.

Appiah-Kubi, 1979: Appiah-Kubi, K. & Torres, S. (eds.) *African Theology en route,* (New York: Orbis Books).

Bediako, Kwame, 1984: 'Biblical Christologies in the context of African Traditional Religions', in Vinay Samuel & Chris Sugden (eds.), *Sharing Jesus in the Two-Thirds World,* (Grand Rapids: Eerdmans), 81-121.

– 1985: 'The Missionary Inheritance', in R. Keeley (ed.), *Christianity—A world faith*, (Tring: Lion Publishing), 303-11.

– 1989: 'The roots of African theology', in *International Bulletin of Missionary Research*, vol. 13, no. 2, April (1989).

– 1990: *Jesus in African Culture–A Ghanaian perspective, (*Accra: Asempa Publishers).

– 1992: *Theology and Identity—The impact of culture upon Christian thought in the second century and modern Africa*, (Oxford: Regnum Books).

Bimwenyi-Kweshi, O., 1984: *Discours théologique négro-africain, (*Paris: Présence Africaine).

p'Bitek, Okot, 1970: *African Religions in Western Scholarship, (*Kampala: East African Literature Bureau).

Bujo, Bénézet, 1992: *African theology in its social context, (*New York: Orbis Books).

Cragg, Kenneth, 1968: *Christianity in World Perspective*, (London: Lutterworth Press).

– 1980: 'Conversion and Convertibility with special reference to Muslims'. in John R.W. Stott & Robert Coote (eds.), *Down to Earth—Studies in Christianity and Culture, (*Grand Rapids: Eerdmans).

Dickson, Kwesi, 1984: *Theology in Africa*, (London/New York: Darton, Longman & Todd/Orbis Books).

Fasholé-Luke, E., 1975: 'The Quest for an African Christian theology', in *The Ecumenical Review, vol. 27, no. 3, (1975), 259-69.

Gaba, Christian R., 1968: 'Sacrifice in Anlo religion—Part I', in *Ghana Bulletin of Theology,* vol. 3, no. 5, (1968), 13-19.
- 1969: 'Sacrifice in Anlo religion—Part II', in *Ghana Bulletin of Theology,* vol. 3, no. 7, (1969), 1-7.
- 1977: *Scriptures of an African people,* (New York: Nok Publications).
Hastings, Adrian, 1976: *African Christianity—An Essay in Interpretation,* (London: Geoffrey Chapman).
- 1989: *African Catholicism—An Essay in Discovery,* (London: SCM Press).
Kibicho, Samuel G., 1978: ' The Continuity of the African conception of God into and through Christianity: A Kikuyu case study', in E. Fasholé-Luke et al. (eds.), *Christianity in Independent Africa,* (London: Rex Collings), 370-88.
Idowu, Bolaji, 1962: *Olódùmarè—God in Yoruba Belief,* (London: Longman).
- 1965: *Towards an Indigenous Church,* (London: OUP).
- 1968: 'The predicament of the Church in Africa', in C.G. Baëta (ed.), *Christianity in Tropical Africa,* (London: OUP), 415-40.
- 1969: 'Introduction' and article, 'God', in Kwesi A. Dickson & Paul Ellingworth (eds.), *Biblical Revelation and African Beliefs,* (London: Lutterworth Press), 9-16; 17-29.
- 1973: *African Traditional Religion—A Definition,* (London: SCM Press).
Kato, Byang H., 1975: *Theological Pitfalls in Africa,* (Kisumu: Evangel Publishing House).
Mazrui, Ali, 1980: *The African Condition—A Political Diagnosis,* (London: Heinemann).
Mbiti, John S., 1970: 'The Future of Christianity in Africa (1970-2000), in *Communio Viatorum: Theological Quarterly,* vol. 13, (1970), 1-2.
- 1970: *New Testament Eschatology in an African Background—A Study of the Encounter between New Testament theology and African Traditional Concepts,* (London: OUP).
- 1972: 'Some African Concepts of Christology', in Georg F. Vicedom (ed.), *Christ and the Younger Churches,* (London: SPCK).
- 1979: 'Cattle are born with ears, their horns grow later: towards an appreciation of African oral theology', in *Africa Theological Journal,* 8(1), (1979), 15-25.
- 1986: *Bible and Theology in African Christianity,* (Nairobi: OUP).
McKenzie, P.R., 1975-76: 'Review of John Mbiti, *The Prayers of African Religion,* in *The Expository Times,* vol. 87, (1975-76), 220-21.
The Missionary Message, 1910: *The Missionary Message in relation to non-Christian religions—The World Missionary Conference 1910—report of Commission IV,* (Edinburgh & London: Oliphant, Anderson & Ferrier).
Mulago gwa Cikala Musharhamina, 1957: *Des prêtres noirs s'interrogent,* (Paris: Les Editions du Cerf).
- 1980: *La Religion Traditionnelle des Bantu et leur vision du monde,* (2ème édition, Bibliothèque du Centre d'Etudes des Religions Africaines, 5), (Kinshasa: Faculté de Théologie Catholique).
Mveng, Engelbert, 1988: 'African Liberation Theology', in L. Boff & V. Elizondo, (eds.), *Third World Theologies—Convergences and Differences,* (Concilium 199), (Edinburgh: T.& T. Clark).
Newbigin, Lesslie, 1986: *Foolishness to the Greeks—The Gospel and Western Culture,* (Geneva: World Council of Churches).
- 1987: 'Can the West be converted?', in *International Bulletin of Missionary Research,* vol. 11, no. 1, January, (1987), 2-7.
- 1989: *The Gospel in a pluralistic society,* (Grand Rapids: Eerdmans).

- (ed.), 1989: *Mission and the crisis of Western culture*, (Edinburgh: Handsel Press).
- 1991: *Truth to tell—the Gospel as Public Truth*, (Grand Rapids: Eerdmans/Geneva: World Council of Churches).

Nyamiti, Charles, 1984: *Christ as our Ancestor—Christology from an African perspective*, (Gweru: Mambo Press).

Okorocha, C.C., 1987: *The Meaning of religious conversion in Africa—The case of the Igbo of Nigeria*, (Avebury: Gower Publishing Co. Ltd).

Pobee, John S., 1979: *Toward an African Theology*, (Nashville: Abingdon Press).

Ray, Benjamin C., 1976: *African Religions—Symbols, Ritual and Community*, (Englewood Cliffs, New Jersey: Prentice Hall Inc).

Sanneh, Lamin, 1983: *West African Christianity—The religious impact*, (London: C. Hurst).

- 1989: *Translating the message—the missionary impact on culture*, (New York: Orbis Books).

Sanon, 1982: Sanon, Anselme T. & Luneau, René, *Enraciner l'Evangile—Initiations africaines et pédagogie de la foi*, (Paris: Les Editions du Cerf).

Sawyerr, Harry, 1968: *Creative Evangelism—Towards a new Christian Encounter with Africa*, (London: Lutterworth Press).

Schreiter, Robert (ed.), 1991: *Faces of Jesus in Africa*, (London: SCM Press).

Setiloane, Gabriel M., 1976: *The Image of God among the Sotho-Tswana*, (Rotterdam: AA Balkema).

- 1978: 'How the Traditional world-view persists in the Christianity of the Sotho-Tswana', in E. Fasholé-Luke et al. (eds.), *Christianity in Independent Africa*, 402-12.

Tiénou, Tite, 1982: 'Biblical Foundations for African Theology', in *Missiology*, vol. 10, no. 4, (1982), 435-48.

Tschibangu, T., 1979: 'The Task of African Theologians', in Appiah-Kubi, K. & Torres, S. (eds.), *African Theology en route*, 73-79.

- 1980: *La théologie comme science au XXème siècle*, (Kinshasa: Faculté de Théologie Catholique).

Tutu, Desmond, 1978: 'Whither African Theology?', in E. Fasholé-Luke et al. (eds.), *Christianity in Independent Africa*, 364-69.

- 1987: 'Black Theology and African Theology—Soulmates or Antagonists?', in Parratt, John (ed.), *A Reader in African Christian Theology*, (London: SPCK).

Verkuyl, Johannes, 1978: *Contemporary Missiology—An Introduction* (ET by Dale Cooper), (Grand Rapids: Eerdmans).

Walls, Andrew F., 1978: 'Africa and Christian Identity', in *Mission Focus*, vol. 6, no. 7, November (1978), 11-13.

- 1996: 'The Gospel as the Prisoner and Liberator of Culture', in *The Missionary Movement in Christian History, Studies in the Transmission of Faith*, (Edinburgh/New York: T. & T. Clark/Orbis Books), 3-15. Also 'Culture and Coherence in Christian History', 16-25; 'The translation principle in Christian history', 26-42; and 'Structural problems in Mission Studies', 146-55.

CHAPTER 5

Africa and the Fathers: The relevance of early Hellenistic Christian theology for modern Africa

The phase of Christian history offering the most instructive parallels to the modern African context is the beginning of Hellenistic Christianity in the early Roman Empire. With Christianity virtually transposed from its original Jewish matrix and fast becoming a predominantly Gentile phenomenon, there emerged from the circles of Gentile Christian thought a significant body of Christian literature, in which the problem of Christian identity and the nature of continuity with the pre-Christian tradition began to be faced in earnest.

Traditionally, early Christian writers have been studied largely for their contribution or otherwise to the development of Christian doctrine. Their careers have tended to be assessed in terms ᴏf their relation to orthodoxy or heresy. However, looked at from the standpoint of the Christian identity problem and how it was faced in relation to the issues raised for the Christian consciousness by Graeco-Roman culture in which they all shared to varying degrees, these writers become interesting in themselves as persons. Their careers gain a significance beyond questions of dogma alone; they become important as witnessess to a more enduring problem: the Christian's response to the religious past as well as to the cultural tradition in which one stands, and the significance of that response for the development of theological answers to the culturally-rooted questions of the context.

Like their counterparts in the African Church of the twentieth century, the Christian writers of the early period manifested the signs of being the product of, and belonging to, a period of transition. They displayed bold initiatives in actual theological production, but were also marked by a certain polemicism and some uncertainty as to their methods of argumentation. With their clearly defined religious convictions, there went a cautious feeling after a sound basis for integrating 'old' and 'new' in the light of their new faith. As with the African context, the reader comes upon material that derives from more than a merely intellectual exercise; confronted with the task of vindicating Christian identity in relation to Graeco-Roman culture which had its own religious and intellectual heritage, they were having to work out that identity in terms of a religious conviction whose very ground of appeal appeared to lie outside of their culture. In the process of the adjustments, adaptations and rejections that took place, some of the formative factors in the Christian theological tradition were clarified and bequeathed to later generations. (Introduction, pp.7-8)

It was also part of the initial impulse for this study to test the explicit suggestion that the question of identity with its significance for the development of theological self-consciousness, constitutes a shared presumption of the formative phase of Hellenistic Christian thought in the second century AD, on the one hand, and the early flowering of Christian theology in the post-missionary Church in twentieth-century Africa, on the other. According to this argument, the question of identity constitutes a 'hermeneutical key' which, by granting access to the concerns exhibited by Christian writers in the two contexts, leads to a deeper understanding of the modern situation in particular, and shows how the modern context manifests features identifiable elsewhere in Christian history. It is now time to assess the extent to which the patristic evidence examined helps to clarify the modern context and contributes positive insights towards a solution of the modern problems.

The point of the correlation suggested here is not that the ancient and the modern contexts are in any sense interchangeable; nor is it implied that the questions and issues involved in the modern situation have been formulated in the same terms as in the earlier context; it is evident that the solutions from the past do not have a direct and unmediated relevance for the problems of the present. Yet it is possible to find in the past, analogues to the situations and circumstances in the present that raise some of the perennial questions that Christian reflection in every age is required to handle (Norris, 1966:vii). By the same token, the answers that were given in the past may illuminate the path of the modern inquirer after solutions to the problems of the present.

'Continuity' and 'Discontinuity': Problems of Meaning

At the end of a wide-ranging survey of the quest for an appropriate Christian theological idiom in modern Africa, E.W. Fasholé-Luke summed up the evidence as follows:

> ... the quest for African Christian theologies which has been vigorously pursued in the last decade, amounts to attempting to make clear the fact that conversion to Christianity must be coupled with cultural continuity. Furthermore, if Christianity is to change its status from that of resident alien to that of citizen, then it must become incarnate in the life and thought of Africa, and its theologies must bear the distinctive stamp of mature African thinking and reflection. What African theologians have been endeavouring to do, is to draw together the various and disparate sources that make up the total religious experience of Christians in Africa into a coherent and meaningful pattern. (Fasholé-Luke, 1975:267-68)

In this statement, Dr. Fasholé-Luke clarifies a significant point of convergence between the circumstances surrounding the birth of modern African theology and those that attended the rise of the Christian theological tradition in Graeco-Roman culture. For it was the interaction of a heightened sense of Christian self-consciousness on the one hand, and the awareness of a shared intellectual heritage in a common culture on the other, that provided the major motivating force for the positive vindication of Christianity in the Graeco-Roman world by early Christian writers. In the case of Justin and Clement of Alexandria, the point is obvious; and yet it has to be maintained with regard to Tatian and Tertullian also, because it is the only basis on which sufficient communication with the cultural context could take place. It is true that in terms of the value placed on the insights derived from the common culture they shared with their non-Christian contemporaries, these four early Christian writers fall into two groups with some considerable differences between them, but these differences are as much the product of temperament, education and background, as of varying perceptions of their cultural world. On the fundamental issue of Christians convictions, their views are strikingly similar, and they remained remarkably unanimous in the essentials of what they affirmed theologically with regard to the 'Syriac' content of the Gospel that had come to them through the religious history of Israel—with its 'Barbarian' elements (Dix, 1953).

Conceivably, the more Hellenically-minded of them could have chosen the Gnostic solution to the problem of identity and the cultural witness of the Church. This would have involved a radical Hellenisation by jettisoning such barbarian elements as Old Testament history and religion: the doctrine of the absolute reality and sovereignty of the one and only Living God as the centre of the universe, as against the rule of the many, postulated from human experience; the doctrine of the Incarnate God; a drastic eschatology and bodily resurrection; the opposition of history to myth in matters of religion; divine revelation as against human speculation. It is extraordinary that this 'Hellenistic' solution did not find favour with Christian thinkers who were as self-consciously Hellenistic as were the Gnostics. The repudiation by the Great Church of both the Marcionite solution to the problem of the canon of Scripture and the Valentinian theology of *aeons* and *ogdoads*, is therefore significant. One can even pursue the distinctions into the controversies of later times. For what became recognised as orthodoxy at Nicaea in AD 325 and found full ratification at Constantinople in AD 381 by a predominantly Hellenistic Church, speaking Greek and thinking in Greek, was in fact the 'Barbarian' philosophy of the Living God of 'Syriac' origin. The 'unknown God' of pre-Christian Athens (Acts 17:23) was now affirmed as the 'One God, Father Almighty, Maker of all things, visible and invisible…'

From the angle of the dynamics of early Christian thought amid Graeco-Roman culture, concepts such as 'continuity' and 'discontinuity' may even be misleading. It is not enough to see Justin and Clement as protagonists of 'continuity' with Tatian and Tertullian representing the opposite tendency of 'discontinuity'. All four writers are clear on the importance of fidelity to the Scriptures and to Christian tradition as handed on from apostolic times. What is even more remarkable, in the context of the conflict of cultures between Hellenism and Barbarism, is the fact that all, including the most Greek of them, Clement of Alexandria, were utterly convinced of the Barbarian character and origins of the Christian revelation, the true and only effectual philosophy; so that they explained 'the headway made in history by the Greek mind' (Jaeger, 1961:35) in terms of borrowings from the more ancient Scriptural tradition, or else, as simply the data of God's self-revelation in Hellenistic tradition.

Tatian, from his vantage point as an Assyrian, and finding the supposed Barbarian philosophy a powerful tool for warding off the alien imposition of a culture in which he did not believe, understandably exploited the argument about borrowings most intensely of all. But Tatian did not thereby become simply a champion of 'discontinuity'; he affirmed another kind of 'continuity', though not with Hellenistic tradition, a continuity with Barbarism as the essential character of the Christian faith. It is most unlikely that Christians of Hellenistic culture would have followed Tatian in his polemic. And yet, paradoxically, the heart of Tatian's anti-Hellenistic polemic, the chronological argument for the priority of Moses and the Old Testament tradition, became his most enduring contribution to the Greek-speaking Church. With the tools that Tatian thus provided, a writer like Clement of Alexandria was able to argue for the antiquity of the Christian tradition, and so to secure for it 'continuity' with a truly ancient and ancestral heritage within a culture that had great respect for pedigree.

Tertullian is the genuine enigma. He must not be set apart from the Greek Apologists, since he and they form an intellectual unity. Tertullian's advance on his Greek counterparts consists in the greater vehemence of his response to the hostile environment and of his defence of Christian self-identity. When it is recognised that the 'discontinuity' which Tertullian postulated was that between the divine revelation granted in Christian tradition on the one hand, and all human speculative systems on the other, his position too becomes more complex. For Tertullian also affirmed a form of 'continuity', a continuity of the Christian's unsullied conscience. There is perhaps no more vigorous exponent of 'the pilgrim principle', which defines Christian authenticity and self-understanding in terms of factors lying outside of one's natural culture and society (Walls, 1996). Yet it is doubtful whether Tertullian would have described his response to his cultural context in *cultural* terms; from Tertullian's standpoint, the Christian's response to the sinful world could only be religious because Christian self-understanding was essentially religious in character. Since all that was of the world was of demons, it followed that the entire outfit sustaining the cultural and political life of the Empire—in other words, everything that lay outside of Christian self-consciousness and of the Christian community thus conceived—was to be rejected. The Christian was to maintain the 'continuity' of a radical alternative religious system and *vision du monde* that ought to be entirely *Christian*.

If the development of early Hellenistic Christian thought on this issue has any value for subsequent Christian history, it may be in what it shows about the complexities that attach to the 'continuity' or 'discontinuity' with every form of pre-Christian tradition. The subject has tended to be oversimplified where the Christian story of modern Africa is concerned:

> The viewpoint of Tertullian the Montanist has been accepted with regard to the indigenous culture [of Africa] while with regard to the Western culture, that of Abelard and the early European approach has been accepted. (Oosthuizen, 1968: 4)

My own study of Tertullian modifies somewhat the traditional perception of his approach, by giving due weight to the essentially religious character of his outlook. However, when the traditional view of Tertullian's position, described as 'Christ against culture' (Niebuhr, 1951:51), is set beside that of Abelard and the early European approach, described as 'Christ of culture' (Niebuhr, 1951:83ff), then Oosthuizen's point becomes clear: the presumption that the Christian Gospel is somehow intrinsically 'part of the Western way of life' has the effect of making suspect all serious attempts at theological indigenisation in Africa (and in any non-Western context). This explains why the efforts of Africa's theologians to 'draw together the various and disparate sources which make up the total religious experience of Christians in Africa into a coherent and meaningful pattern' (Fasholé-Luke, 1975:268), have tended to be met with scepticism. Yet, as our ancient analogues in early Hellenistic Christian thought show, a positive evaluation of the pre-Christian tradition and an attempt to derive insights from it for the declaration of Christian convictions need not imply a theological syncretism. Of our African writers—all committed churchmen—none, in giving a positive evaluation of the pre-Christian African tradition, sees it as antithetical to the significance of the Christian Gospel for Africa. In the case of Byang Kato, the one writer who maintained a negative and unsympathetic approach to every form of 'non-Christian' religion, we have had reason to question the theological basis of his outlook (Kato, 1975).

Some specific areas of relevance: (a) The possibility of synthesis

One aspect of the relevance of the achievement of early Hellenistic Christian thought for the modern African context has to do, therefore, with the possibility of a genuine theology that seeks a synthesis between Christian religious commitment and cultural continuity. This conclusion was clearly stated

by André Benoit, who included a discussion of the value of patristic studies
for the 'Younger Churches' in his discussion of the relevance of the Church
Fathers for the Church in the twentieth century:

> It is a question for them of rethinking Christianity within the framework
> of a non-Western culture without, however, betraying or twisting it. That is
> to say that they must recover the usable elements in the native civilisations
> and reject the others. The Fathers did the same. As bearers of the Gospel
> they had to express it within the framework of Hellenistic culture; they
> preserved the usable elements of that culture and left aside what was with-
> out value. Studying the Fathers would in this case render appreciable
> service in emphasising the fundamental elements of all Christian theology
> and in showing the necessity for a certain amount of adaptation as well as
> the limits to it. (Benoit, 1961:79)

If Benoit is right that the theology of the Fathers manifests 'fundamental
elements of all Christian theology', then one of these is the fact that no Christian theology in any age is simply a repetition of the inherited Christian tradition; all Christian theology is a synthesis, an 'adaptation' of the inherited
Christian tradition in the service of new formulations of the problem of 'the
life of the universe and the life of man considered in relation to the will and
purpose of the Creator', the subject matter of theology (Casserley, 1952:73).

(b) The Challenge of Pluralism

The ancient achievement in early Hellenistic Christianity is also significant
for our modern concerns in view of the context in which it took place. Benoit
noted this point also, though he limited its value to similarities between the
'paganism' that confronted the Early Church and the 'paganism' that the
'Younger Churches' have to encounter in their cultural world (Benoit, 1961:
78-79). In the light of studies in the phenomenology of religion, one can clarify further these suggestions about the similarities in the respective 'pagan-
isms' in the contexts of early Hellenistic Christianity and the modern
'Younger Churches'. Not only has the expansion of Christianity registered
its most marked responses in 'societies with primal religious systems,' (Walls,
1978) but also this peculiar historical connection between this form of
'paganism' and Christianity raises questions about possible 'affinities
between the Christian and primal traditions' (Turner, 1977:37) which have
hitherto not been taken seriously (Walls, 1978:11).
    However, what Benoit failed to indicate was that the really important point
of convergence between these ancient and the modern contexts, consisted in
the fact and the experience of pluralism. Long before pluralism, religious as
well as cultural, became a subject of serious discussion in the Western world,

many Christian communities in Africa had been living, witnessing and learning to survive and grow in the context of religious pluralism. Unlike Western Europe, 'generally speaking Africa has avoided *Christian* ontocracies' (Walls, 1976:187), whereby throne and altar were integrated (van Leeuwen, 1964). In the modern African 'pluralism of Christian and Muslim, or of Christianity and adherents of the old religion, or of different and sometimes competing forms of Christianity' (Walls, 1976:187), it is clear that theology cannot be done, studied and taught in the same way as in the Western European tradition, where the challenge of pluralism was virtually unknown or was minimal for a very long time. It also means that the intellectual framework as well as the kind of questions that will be posed, will differ from those that have characterised the Western European tradition in theology.

c) Theology as Indigenisation

The shifts in interests that almost every one of Africa's theologians, trained in theology according to a Western model, has been 'forced' to make is symptomatic of the fact that both the content of theological study and the agenda for the African theological enterprise were developing along lines that could not have been anticipated from the Western missionary background of the churches in Africa. An indication of the radically new situation is the fact that the university faculties of Divinity or Theology that had developed within European Christendom with their attention directed towards the investigation of the traditional fields of biblical, historical and dogmatic studies, have had to make way for departments of Religious Studies with a more pronounced interest in the phenomenology and theology of religions. No self-respecting theological institution in Africa can avoid the study of African Traditional Religions. Not only are they 'at the very centre of the academic stage' (Hastings, 1976:183), the 'conditions of a plural society where religion is a massive, unignorable fact of life' (Walls, 1980:144), demand it. Paradoxically, this also means that for modern Africa's theologians, inheritors of nearly twenty centuries of Christian scholarship, the theological task becomes more, rather than less exacting (Walls, 1976:184).

In this regard also, the achievement of early Hellenistic Christian theology has a relevance for the modern African context. The Apostolic Fathers were witnesses to the traditional faith rather than interpreters of it (Kelly, 1968:90). But from Justin Martyr onwards, new questions and issues were forced upon the growing, largely Hellenistic, Church. How did the Gospel relate to the Hellenistic past? What was the nature of the saving activity of the one Living God through the centuries prior to the Incarnation of the Saviour and inauguration of the Christian era, or (as Clement of Alexandria chose to call it) the 'common tradition', the era of 'the universal calling to salvation by the one Lord and Saviour of all mankind'? Justin was convinced that there were Christians before Christ, and he was prepared to offer names as evidence for the truth of his intuition. Clement went even further and argued that some philosophers and thoughtful persons of the past had in fact found justification through their genuine quest after nobler conceptions of the divine and excellence in conduct; that the philosophical tradition itself was a divine gift bestowed upon Hellenistic culture to lead to Christ and so to serve much the same purpose as the Old Testament revelation in the religious history of the Hebrews.

Some elements in this new Christian thinking about the pre-Christian tradition seemed far removed from the New Testament, and some Christians sought to remind Clement of St. Paul's warning about the dangers of philosophy (Colossians 2:8). Clement had a ready response: the apostle did not mean all philosophy, but only the Epicurean sort, which had no room for God and exalted pleasure as the fundamental principle of life. All philosophical tenets were to be tested, and those that approximated to Christian beliefs integrated into Christian theology; in fact, in so far as they approximated to Christian convictions, they were borrowings from the Scriptures, or were the outcome and evidence of direct inspiration by God in Hellenistic tradition.

The really striking feature in this patristic reinterpretation of the pre-Christian religious tradition is the extent to which it was rooted in the quest for an integral picture of the redemptive activity of God, in view of the fact that God is one and universal; but this integral picture of the divine activity was also necessary for an integrated Christian self-consciousness within Hellenistic culture (Luneau, 1967). Therefore, the effort to trace a salvific dimension in the pre-Christian tradition and by implication to identify 'Christian' antecedents in it, answered to a single urge, that of articulating a unified world-picture in which the God of Christian revelation was seen to be Who He really is: the one and only God of all mankind. In this the patristic thought was the authentic heir of the theology of St. Paul (Romans 3:29f; 10:11-13).

d) The pre-Christian heritage as a 'tradition of response'

By adopting this open and inclusive approach to the pre-Christian tradition, Justin and Clement were refusing to treat Christian revelation and the 'non-Christian' tradition as mutually exclusive systems. Rather, in their thinking, the encounter between the two realities took place on quite different terms, in the realm of spirit, and they were prepared to argue for the operation of the pre-incarnate Word in the 'non-Christian' tradition no less than in the Christian. Looked at from this angle, the pre-Christian tradition became a 'tradition of response' to the reality of the Transcendent (Taylor, 1972:182ff), and could be probed not so much for the measure of truth it contained, as for the truth of the human response to the divine action within the tradition. Consequently, the postulate of 'two traditions' within the Hellenistic heritage, the true and the false, could be called the postulate of 'two responses'. The early Christian apologists' instinct to welcome and identify with the philosophical tradition and to reject the popular religion and its mythology, finds its deepest meaning here. However, in making common cause with philosophy, they were still operating within a unified framework of the religious quests of their time, since the philosophy they meant was virtually a religion—the religion of educated and thoughtful people. The fact that the African heritage does not seem to have produced a distinct tradition of 'philosophy' independent of religion, need not hamper the usefulness of the relevant patristic insights at this point. The efforts of Idowu, Mbiti and Mulago to demonstrate, on the basis of the oneness of God and the pre-Christian African sense of God, that African Christian experience is not totally discontinuous with the pre-Christian heritage, fall within the approach to the Hellenistic heritage adopted by Justin and Clement. Besides, the fact that in both the early Hellenistic and modern African contexts, the solution of the problem posed by the pre-Christian tradition is invariably related to the question of identity, shows the extent to which the two contexts shed light on each other.

Nevertheless, it remains true that the positive evaluation of the African pre-Christian heritage has, on the whole, said 'little … about the failings of the past (on the African side)' (Hastings, 1976:52). Even though John Mbiti has acknowledged the existence of 'deadness and rottenness in our traditional religiosity' which must be purged by the Christian faith as professed by Africans (Mbiti, 1970:436-37), the theme is not developed by him, nor by the other writers who give a positive interpretation of Africa's 'old' religions. A possible reason may be that African theology so far has been concerned mainly to respond to the derogatory European evaluation of African tradition by seeking to achieve a genuinely sympathetic interpretation of the religious past. In the process, Africa's theologians were in fact providing the kind of 'theological and scholarly stiffening for the new African Church which was important in the establishment of confidence' (Hastings, 1979:231). On the other hand, it may indicate something of a methodological problem in African theology that the blemishes of the religious past have not so far been adequately clarified and set in perspective. Unlike the Fathers who inherited from their pre-Christian background a tradition of intellectual critique of the old religion that was affirmative of their cultural identity, Africa's theologians received a critique that was extraneous and Eurocentric and could only be alienating for them and destructive of the very concept of an African theology of synthesis. Here the weakness noted in the theological outlook of Byang Kato finds its deepest significance. Here also we find the reason why the task of articulating the theological significance of the pre-Christian religious tradition is likely to remain a preoccupation of African theology for some time yet (Tshibangu, 1979). In the process, it may be that the patristic experiments in the early centuries of the Christian movement will find a more prominent place in the consciousness of Africa's theologians and the 'Tertullianic' tendency that Byang Kato represented may need to be taken more seriously, even if his own solution was far from adequate.

Indeed, it is curious that those of Africa's theologians who have sought to give a positive evaluation of the pre-Christian heritage have hardly made any conscious or systematic use of the patristic insights we have considered. John Mbiti, whose outlook and approach come the closest to those of Justin and Clement, nowhere mentions them in this connection. Mulago, whose Catholic theological training exposed him to the patristic literature most intimately of all, treats the Fathers merely as part of the *magisterium* of the Church and does not draw upon their significance for his own concern with a theology of synthesis. Interestingly, it was Byang Kato who noted the parallels between the context of the Hellenistic Church of the second century and that of the African Church of the twentieth century; but he then went on to reject the theological achievement of early Hellenistic Christianity. Thus, whilst African theology has been wrestling with the same problems as confronted early Hellenistic Christian theology (Walls, 1996:14), African theologians have pursued their modern agenda, so far at least, in isolation from the most relevant analogue in the history of Christian thought.

In one sense this is a disturbing state of affairs; it obscures the true character of the achievement of African theology which is thereby consigned to a sort of limbo, with no clear links to the historical tradition of Christian theological reflection. As a consequence, African theology's properly *theological* concern with the African pre-Christian heritage has tended to be assessed by the criteria of social anthropology, and so has been generally misunderstood. Yet it is the history of Christian theological thought, and the early patristic phase of that history in particular, that most adequately clarifies its intuitions and illuminates its insights.

Agenda for the future: (a) African theology and its African critics

It is also the early patristic experiments that most helpfully identify crucial areas still requiring attention in modern African theology. The fact that African theology has yet to produce a full-scale response to Okot p'Bitek, 'the authentic voice of Celsus' (Walls,1996:13) in our modern context, and other African non-Christian critics of the African theological enterprise, may indicate the strength of his criticism that by seeking to 'christianise' the African religious past, African theology is merely 'continuing the missionary misrepresentation of the past' (p'Bitek, 1966; 1970). It may also reveal a more fundamental lack that needs to be addressed in the agenda of the future.

African theology has now overturned virtually every negative verdict passed on African tradition by the ethnocentricism of the Western missionary enterprise. In the process, African theology has provided the theoretical validation for the 'massive and unignorable fact and factor' of Christianity 'in the African scene' as a genuinely African reality (Baëta, 1968). But African theology is now called upon to engage creatively with the developing African intellectual opinion that interprets African reality differently, to the point of setting aside the very principle of religion itself (Wiredu, 1980). Here a basic postulate of the entire modern African theological enterprise is challenged, namely, the view that African existence and African interpretations of that existence are essentially and totally *religious*. How African Theology responds to this *African* philosophical and intellectual atheism must certainly be one of the crucial issues in the theology of the future.

b) The Christian Faith as 'a historical category' in the African experience

However, the response to this new African challenge will form part of a much wider task that involves clarifying in African experience what Marcel Simon meant when he described the emergence of Christianity in the ancient world as the 'birth of a historical category' (Simon, 1981). For the response to Celsus in early Hellenistic Christian theology that came through Origen was the culmination of a process of Christian self-definition in Graeco-Roman culture (Chadwick, 1980:ix). In the same way, it is as the modern African Christian identity problem is fully thought through that the definitive response to the non-Christian African critics of African theology can be given.

Here, the relevance of the patristic achievement consists in the way they managed to preserve the Christian revelation intact against those who would have divested it of its 'Barbarian' character, and yet were able to vindicate for the Christian conscience a place to feel at home in the culture they shared with their non-Christian contemporaries. But at the heart of that achievement was their perception of the Gospel itself —how they understood 'the specific nature of Christianity' (Simon, 1981:335). In this regard, our ancient analogue shades into an ancient model and reveals the Fathers as truly our masters. For in the thinking of the early Christian writers, the Christian Gospel came to constitute an intellectual and historical category in its own right; it not only provided them with a precious interpretative key for discerning the religious meanings inherent in their heritage, so that they could decide what to accept and what to reject; in the Gospel they also found an all-encompassing reality and an overall integrating principle that enabled them to understand themselves and their past, and face the future, because the Gospel of Jesus Christ became for them the heir to all that was worthy in the past, whilst it held all the potential of the future.

As Baëta has observed regarding Christianity in Africa:

> In numberless institutions of many different kinds as well as in the equally numerous and diverse voluntary organisations and free associations of

men, women and children; in the pervasive influence and challenge of its message to men and demand upon their individual lives and their relationships with one another; in countless personal and group decisions made, and lives actually lived very differently from what they would otherwise have been; in the new high hopes and aspirations for individual and social destiny which it has awakened; in the sheer excellence of human performance in devotion and courageous, self-sacrificing service to others, and yet in other ways, Christianity ... plays a role and exerts a force in tropical Africa which is none the less real or significant because it eludes full and conclusive analysis. (Baëta, 1968: xii-xiii)

The truth of Baëta's observation may well be illustrated in the following incident of religious encounter reported from Ghana:

A sharp conflict recently erupted between the Christian churches and the traditional authorities in the Ghanaian town of Akim Tafo over violation by the churches of a ban on drumming during a traditional religious festival. During the two weeks preceding the Ohum religious festival, drumming, clapping of hands, wailing, firing of musketry, and any other noises likely to disturb the gods is not permitted. But Christian churches in the town ignored the ban and continued to allow drumming during their worship services, arguing that drumming was an essential part of the Ghanaian form of worship. ('Drumbeat in Church', *Voice Weekly,* 3-9 Sept. 1980:6)

From a religious point of view, the most striking thing about this incident is that the controversy took place in the context of worship. Here is a classic instance of power-encounter, a meeting of experiences, an interaction of apprehensions of reality. What is even more interesting about this religious conflict is the fact that the Christians, as concerned as their non-Christian opponents to affirm their cultural integrity, insist that their *Christian* worship with the aid of drums, even though it may be in violation of a traditional religious ban, has an equal right to being recognised as authentic *Ghanaian* worship.

Here Christian history comes full circle, and, as in our ancient analogue, the 'tradition of response' bifurcates, not because the Gospel introduces an entirely new religious system unrelated to the cultural heritage (otherwise the Christians of Akim Tafo could hardly claim against the devotees of the 'old' gods that their Christian worship was in any real sense Ghanaian). Rather, the Gospel of Jesus Christ, turning as it does 'on grace and personality' and having 'to do with men as men, their sins and their fears, and not with Jews as Jews, or Greeks as Greeks' (Cragg, 1968:48), introduces a historical category which by transcending the stubborn human divisions of race, culture and lineage, not only provides a means of making manifest the dynamic of spirituality for what it is, but also clarifies in a new way the nature of identity as ultimately rooted in God and Christ. In the words of John Mbiti (Mbiti, 1973:94):

> Cultural identities are temporary, serving to yield us as Christians to the fullness of our identity with Christ. Paradoxically, culture snatches us away from Christ, it denies that we are His; yet when it is best understood, at its meeting with Christianity, culture drives us to Christ and surrenders us to Him, affirming us to be permanently, totally and unconditionally His own.

Perhaps nothing demonstrates more clearly that the theological achievement of early Hellenistic Christianity in the second century and the emergent theological self-consciousness of African Christianity in the twentieth century, belong to one and the same story.

References

Baëta, C.G. (ed.), 1968: *Christianity in Tropical Africa* (Studies presented and discussed at the 7th International African Seminar, University of Ghana, April, 1965), (London: OUP).

Benoit, André, 1961: *L'actualité des Pères de l'Eglise* (Cahiers théologiques, 47), (Neuchâtel: Editions Delachaux et Niestlé).

p'Bitek, Okot, 1966: *Song of Lawino,* (Nairobi: East African Publishing House).

– 1970: *African Religions in Western Scholarship*, (Kampala: East African Literature Bureau).

Casserley, J.V. Langmead, 1952: *The Retreat from Christianity in the Modern World* (The Maurice Lectures for 1951), (London: Longmans, Green & Co.).

Chadwick, Henry, 1980: *Origen: Contra Celsum,* (Cambridge: CUP).

Cragg, Kenneth, 1968: *Christianity in World Perspective*, (London: Lutterworth Press).

Dix, Gregory, 1953: *Jew and Greek—A Study in the Primitive Church*, (London: Dacre Press, Westminster).

Fasholé-Luke, E.W., 1975: 'The quest for an African Christian theology', in *The Ecumenical Review*, vol. 27, no.3, July, (1975) 259-69.

Hastings, Adrian, 1976: *African Christianity: An essay in interpretation*, (London: Geoffrey Chapman).

– 1979: *A History of African Christianity 1950-1975*, (Cambridge: CUP).

Jaeger, Werner, 1961: *Early Christianity and Greek Paideia*, (London: OUP).

Kato, Byang, 1975: *African Cultural Revolution and the Christian Faith*, (Jos: Challenge Publications).

– 1975: *Theological Pitfalls in Africa*, (Kisumu: Evangel Publishing House).

Kelly, J.N.D., 1968: *Early Christian Doctrines* (4th ed), (London: A. & C. Black).

Leeuwen, Arend Th. van, 1964: *Christianity in World History, The Meeting of the Faiths of East and West* (ET by H.H. Hoskins), (London: Edinburgh House Press).

Luneau, A., 1967: 'Pour aider au dialogue: les Pères et les religions non-chrétiennes, in *Nouvelle Revue Théologique*, Sept—Nov., (1967), 821-41.

Mbiti, John, 1970: 'Christianity and Traditional Religions in Africa', in *International*

Review of Mission, vol. 59, no. 236, October, (1970), 430-40.

– 1973: 'African Indigenous Culture in relation to Evangelism and Church development', in R. Pierce Beaver (ed.), *The Gospel and Frontier Peoples* (A Report of a Consultation, December 1972), (Pasadena: William Carey Library).

Niebuhr, H. Richard, 1951: *Christ and Culture*, (New York: Harper Colophon Books).

Norris, Richard A., 1966: *God and World in early Christian Theology —A Study in Justin Martyr, Irenaeus, Tertullian and Origen*, (London: A. & C. Black).

Oosthuizen, G. C., 1968: *Post-Christianity in Africa—A theological and anthropological study*, (London: Hurst & Co).

Simon, Marcel, 1981: 'Christianisme: naissance d'une catégorie historique', in M. Simon, *Le Christianisme et son contexte religieux – Scripta varia* (vol. 1), Wissenschaftliche Untersuchungen zum Neuen Testament, 23, Tübingen: J. C. B. Mohr, 312-35.

Taylor, John V., 1972: *The Go-Between God: the Holy Spirit and the Christian Mission,* (London: SCM Press).

Tshibangu, T., 1979: 'Les tâches de la théologie africaine', in Appiah-Kubi, K., et al (eds.), *Libération ou Adaptation: La Théologie africaine s'interroge*, (Le Colloque d'Accra), (Paris: Editions Harmattan), 92-102.

Turner, H.W., 1977: 'The Primal Religions of the world and their study', in Hayes, Victor (ed.), *Australian Essays in World Religions*, (Bedford Park: Australian Association for World Religions), 27-37.

Walls, A.F., 1976: 'Towards understanding Africa's place in Christian history', in J.S. Pobee (ed.), *Religion in a Pluralistic Society* (Essays presented to Professor C.G. Baëta), (Leiden: E. J. Brill), 180-89.

– 1978: 'Africa and Christian Identity', in *Mission Focus*, vol. 4, no. 7, November, (1978), 11-13.

– 1980: 'A Bag of Needments for the road: Geoffrey Parrinder and the study of religion in Britain', in *Religion*, vol. 10, Autumn, (1980), 141-50.

– 1996: 'The Gospel as the Prisoner and Liberator of Culture', in *The Missionary Movement in Christian History*, (New York/Edinburgh: Orbis Books/T. & T. Clark), 3-15.

Wiredu, Kwasi, 1980: *Philosophy and an African Culture*, (Cambridge: CUP).

CHAPTER 6

One Song in Many Tongues

This chapter takes off from the arguments in my book, *Theology and Identity. The impact of culture upon Christian thought in the second century and modern Africa* (Bediako, 1992), and from a paper entitled, 'How is Jesus Christ Lord? Towards a flexible Christology in a pluralist context' (Bediako, 1996, see Chapter 3), in which I responded to an editorial comment in *Studies in World Christianity* by Professor James Mackey, calling for a 'flexible Christology' that was open to new cultural and theological explorations emerging from circles of non-Western Christianity (Mackey, 1995).

To take these thoughts further, I interact with a paper of Dr. Ken Ross (then of the University of Malawi), on: 'Nicene Methodology and the Christological task in Africa today' (Ross, 1996), in which he sought to show that for the christological task in Africa today, there are some pertinent lessons to learn from the way the Nicene Fathers argued to establish what became accepted as orthodoxy. He focused his discussion particularly on the achievement of Athanasius, identifying a strong link between the Nicene argument of Athanasius against Arius, and the Bible-reading, Bible-believing and worshipping community of the contemporary Church.

Against this evidence on the patristic side, Dr. Ross placed what he regarded as worrying evidence from modern Africa where academic christological explorations seemed to be proceeding in isolation from the life of the church. In fairness to Dr. Ross's argument, there are several African theologians whom he could cite in support of his argument. Charles Nyamiti has stated emphatically: 'None of the existing African Christologies has had any appreciable influence in the life of the African churches...' (Nyamiti, 1992:18) Presumably this includes Nyamiti's own christology, as one who devoted a whole book to the theme of Christ as Ancestor (1984).

The title of Nyamiti's book gives a clue to Dr. Ross's worry, namely that so much of the contemporary christological discussion from Africa is around images of Christ as Ancestor, Healer, Nganga, Chief, Master of Initiation, thereby making the Bible and biblical vocabulary and concepts much less the currency of African Christology. In order to demonstrate the erroneous nature of this trend in African christological discussion, he produced the result of a field survey in northern Malawi in which 420

Christians were asked to choose, out of eight possible titles, which three 'best describe who Jesus is'.

Dr. Ross comments on the results as follows:

> It is striking to notice how frequently the biblical titles for Jesus Christ, such as 'Saviour' or 'Messiah' were preferred to titles derived from the African tradition such as 'ancestor' or 'chief'. ... [I]t could be interpreted in terms of a community being drawn to biblical vocabulary and conceptuality as a means of accurately stating what it has to say about the reality of Jesus Christ. A comparable development in patristic theology would be the way in which the initial natural inclination to understand Jesus in terms of the 'Word' (Logos) gradually gave way to the more biblical 'Son' as it was found that only in this way could justice be done to the relational understanding of God which was found in the Gospel of Jesus Christ. So in African Christology, it may well be that the categories which at first seem to make sense of Jesus in African terms gradually give way to the more biblical categories ...It may be that we are entering a time when biblical vocabulary and concepts are no less indigenous than those derived from African tradition.

I am in sympathy with much of Dr. Ross's paper. My major query is with how he arrives at his conclusions. He does not indicate the language used for this survey, nor in what language the 'biblical categories' were conveyed in the interviews. Since he aims to establish the primacy of African perceptions of Jesus through Bible reading at the grassroots, it would have been interesting to know what the equivalents of the biblical titles for Jesus are in local languages, and then to explore the resonances of those local equivalents.

Since Dr. Ross did not pose the questions in these terms, we should not assume so easily that African Christians will simply prefer biblical titles such as 'Saviour' and 'Messiah' to titles derived from African tradition such as 'ancestor' or 'chief'. 'Messiah' presents peculiar difficulties, since it tends to figure in many languages as a loan-word. 'Chief' and 'ancestor' are rather interesting. In my experience in Ghana, hardly anyone will pray in English to 'Ancestor Jesus' or 'Chief Jesus', but many will pray in Akan to 'Nana Yesu'. 'Nana' means 'ancestor' and is the title for ancestors (and chiefs).

This simple illustration shows us how much more subtle and nuanced the discussion needs to be in this area, for it means that the valencies of 'biblical concepts' and 'biblical vocabulary' are not established simply by word equivalents. For example, of the two terms, 'Word' (Logos) and 'Son' when applied to Jesus, can we say the second is more biblical in view of the prehistory of the first in Greek philosophy? Indeed, is that the important question? Is 'Nana Yesu' less biblical because 'Nana' translates 'Ancestor' in English? Is not the question rather, whether the experience of the reality and actuality of Jesus as intended in Christian affirmation, can inhabit the world of 'Nana' in the same way that it could inhabit the Greek world of 'Logos'? In this specific case, even though 'Nana' recalls the category of 'Ancestor' and in that sense translates the term, in actual fact it is not adequate to leave it at that. For whereas 'Ancestor' is a generic term in English, 'Nana' is both a title and a personal name, in the same way, incidentally, that 'Christos' (Christ) was both a title and a personal name in early Christian usage. All this means that, in fact, 'Nana' is a more satisfactory term for speaking of the actuality of Christ than 'Ancestor'. It should be clear that the real theological problem here has to do with the English word, 'Ancestor', and not with 'Nana'. Indeed, the matter should not be about words and their equivalents at all, but about discerning and recognising what is happening creatively in the context as people encounter, live out and attempt to express their experience of the reality and actuality of Jesus Christ.

This example from contemporary African Christianity recalls parallel developments within the New Testament itself, as I have hinted already in my reference to the use of 'Logos' for Jesus, and as Andrew Walls has pointed out (Walls, 1997). As the early preachers 'started to speak of Kyrios Jesus, parallel to Kyrios Serapis' (Walls, 1997:184), and that 'act of metaphysical translation' was inevitably followed by 'explanation, qualification, supplementation and definition as the identity of Jesus was explored in terms of Hellenistic language and thought', it is as though 'the full stature of Christ becomes attainable' as the Gentiles enter the community, 'as though Christ himself grows as he penetrates Gentile thought and society in the persons of his people', as though the full stature of Christ is revealed only as a fresh cultural entity is incorporated into the Church which is his body.

This is why the exegesis of biblical words and texts may not be taken as completed when one has established meanings in Hebrew, Aramaic and Greek; why, instead, the process needs to continue into all possible languages in which biblical faith is received, mediated and expressed. If this makes the task infinitely more difficult than any one person or group of persons can achieve, it shows all the more how tentative, provisional and contextual all theological efforts are. It becomes even more important with the increasing significance of non-Western Christianity, and the fact that it poses all sorts of questions and produces a whole range of problems for which our theological knowledge, gained through study in the West, has not prepared us.

Does this mean that in researching non-Western Christianity, we are cast adrift on an entirely uncharted sea, with no guiding instruments of any sort? I would suggest that this is not the case. In *Theology and Identity*, I worked with the methodological principle, taken from H.W. Turner, that 'the nature of the field of study must provide the major control over the methods employed' (Turner, 1981:1). On this principle, a most helpful way of understanding developments within African Christian theology was to situate them in continuum with the historical movement that has produced and is likely to produce Christian theology, that is, Christian history. Within Christian history, I found the second to the early third centuries particularly fruitful. There I found some of the more helpful 'ancient analogues' as I called them, for understanding parallel developments in modern Africa.

In the growing endeavour to relate modern developments to ancient analogues, some fine-tuning may be needed. Andrew Walls has identified three stages in the conversion process of the Hellenistic world of thought (Walls, 1997:149). The first stage, the missionary stage, is represented by Paul, most open and accommodating of missionaries, who, understanding that the meanings of Christ extended beyond the vocabulary of Judaism, was open to and indeed began to transpose those meanings into Hellenistic categories, preparing the way for the second stage, the convert stage.

This stage is well represented by Justin Martyr and his immediate successors and imitators. Justin, taking his cue from Paul, explores the Hellenistic meanings of Christ beyond Paul, but only because 'Justin's struggle is outside Paul's experience, for though Paul has known the Hellenistic world from his youth, he lives in it essentially as an outsider' (Walls, 1997:149). Justin's struggle is that of 'identity: how to maintain his Christian identity within the Hellenistic intellectual identity, which he could not abandon because it had shaped his life and his mind.' It is into that world and identity that he must bring Christ. While he fully acknowledges the perversions of that world, Justin nonetheless through his understanding of the Scriptures and his own experience of the living Christ, is convinced that Christ can inhabit that world and work to transform it.

The third stage identified by Andrew Walls, the refiguration or translation stage, is well represented by Origen. This stage could come only beyond the convert stage in a generation that had 'grown up in the Christian faith, was reconciled to its pre-Christian inheritance and was not afraid of either' (Walls, 1997:149). It is following the refiguration stage, the effort to refigure the entire Greek intellectual and scientific inheritance in Christian terms, that the classical developments that we associate with the early church—doctrines, creeds and formulae—could take place, from the materials of the Greek intellectual world and by means of its methods.

Since this formative period is becoming increasingly critical as providing historical paradigms for understanding subsequent periods of Christian history, I find this outline particularly insightful for our present discussion. To return to modern Africa, in *Theology and Identity*, I argued that modern Africa was not as well served by the Western missionary movement as it could have been. Partly because Western missionaries seemed to accept the general Western image of non-Western people, and of Africans in particular, and partly because of their own human frailties, the missionary stage for Africa was not quite as liberative as the apostolic precedent had been for the Hellenistic world. Indeed, one writer, South African missiologist, G.C. Oosthuizen, put it emphatically: 'Africa had no Paul' (Oosthuizen, 1968:235).

If my reading of the evidence is correct, it also helps us appreciate how the convert stage could also become somewhat unclear. I say so because, in my view, African Christian thought is currently at this convert stage, and so the convert stage of the Hellenistic period gives the best clues to the intellectual efforts in African Christology. By relating his discussion of current African Christology to Nicene methodology, Ken Ross may be drawing on a less helpful analogue.

I am not suggesting here that these 'stages' are cast-iron categories, that make different analogical relationships unwarranted. Yet if we are to use historical paradigms and analogous data, it is important to identify the more helpful ones. This brings me back to the initial observations regarding a 'flexible christology'. It should be clear by now that a 'flexible christology' does not have to mean an unrecognisable christology, unrecognisable, that is, within the tradition of the community of faith. On the contrary, since the reflection about Christ is to be carried on in the interface of reading and hearing the Scriptures and experiencing the actuality of Christ in the life-situations of believers, the necessary constraints will also be in operation to ensure that the result is recognisable and owned by the world Christian community.

However, since we are dealing with a translatable faith and translated Scriptures, mother-tongues, new languages, and the potential of new idioms become central and are crucial in the opening up of fresh insights into our common understanding of Christology. On this side of the modern missionary movement and its intense commitment to Scripture translation, we may be tempted to take the subject for granted. We now recognise the critical impact that the Scriptures in the mother-tongues of converts have had in the spread of the Christian faith (Stine, 1990; Sanneh, 1989). But it is important to recognise that it is the modern expansion of the faith into the non-Western world that has alerted us to this phenomenon. What remains to happen, is the realisation that this major event can have a significant impact in the actual Christian idiom in which we articulate our experience. In relation to Africa, Lamin Sanneh has argued that 'Scripture translation imbued local cultures with eternal significance and endowed African languages with a transcendent range' (Sanneh, 1983:166). This means also that African pre-Christian religions had a theological significance in the whole process, for the centrality of Scripture translation points to the significance of local religions for providing the idiom for Christian apprehension in the new languages and cultures in which Christian faith now finds a home.

The significance of the second century and its convert stage in relation to the impact of culture on Christian thought in modern Africa, is the light it throws on the processes involved in the shaping of Christian affirmation in the new cultural contexts and in cultural idioms of Africa in which biblical faith is now being expressed. For in this task, the early Christian Fathers of the second century are truly our masters. They made the Gospel their own to such an extent that it became for them a key to interpret the religious meanings inherent in their heritage, so that they could decide what to accept and what to reject. The Gospel was for them also an all-encompassing reality and principle of integration that enabled them to understand themselves and their past and to face the future, because the Gospel of Jesus Christ became for them the heir to all that was worthy in the past, whilst it held all the potential of the future.

The study of non-Western Christianity needs to show a similarly deepening awareness of the impact of culture on Christian thought, and to pay greater attention to the contribution that the new languages of Christian experience make to the development of Christian thought. Here we anticipate the vision, in the last book of the Bible, of what the Church will look like at the end: the crowd from every nation, tribe, people and language, standing before the throne of God and singing, in their varied languages, the one new song of praise and adoration to the one Saviour of all the redeemed, the Lamb of God, Jesus Christ the Lord (Revelation 7:9).

References

Bediako, Kwame, 1992: *Theology and Identity, The impact of culture upon Christian Thought in the Second Century and Modern Africa*, (Oxford: Regnum Books).

Bediako, Kwame, 1996: a modified verson was published as 'Christ is Lord: How is Jesus Christ unique in the midst of other religious faiths?', in *Exchange—Journal of Missiological and Ecumenical Research*, Vol. 25, No. 1, (1996), 27-41.

Mackey, James, 1995: 'Can Western Christology prove more flexible? Join a family rather than rule an empire', *Studies in World Christianity*, Vol. 1, No. 2, (1995), iii-x.

Nyamiti, Charles, 1992: 'African Christologies Today', in R. J. Schreiter (ed.), *Faces of Jesus in Africa, (*London: SCM Press).

Oosthuizen, G.C., 1968: *Post-Christianity in Africa, A theological and anthropological study*, (London: C. Hurst).

Ross, Kenneth R., 1996: ''Nicene Methodology and the Christological Task in Africa Today', paper given at the Centre for the Study of Christianity in the Non-Western World, University of Edinburgh, 3 December 1996.

Sanneh, Lamin, 1989: *Translating the Message, the Missionary Impact on Culture,* (New York: Orbis Books).

– 1983: 'The Horizontal and Vertical in Mission: An African Perspective', in *International Bulletin of Missionary Research*, Vol. 7, No. 4, October, (1983), 165-71.

Stine, Philip C., 1990: *Bible Translation and the Spread of the Church—the last two hundred years,* (Leiden: E. J. Brill).

Turner, H.W., 1981: 'The way forward in the religious study of African primal religions', in *Journal of Religion in Africa*, Vol. XII, Fasc. 1, (1981), 1-15.

Walls, Andrew F., 1997: 'Old Athens and New Jerusalem: Some signposts for Christian scholarship in the early history of Mission Studies', in *International Bulletin of Missionary Research*, Vol. 21, No. 4, October, (1997), 146-53.

III. Africa and the History of Christianity

CHAPTER 7

The Primal imagination and the opportunity for a new theological idiom

Introduction: Prophet Harris

> One man preached the Gospel in West Africa for nine years and only converted 52. But another man preached the same Gospel just for two years and 120,000 adult West Africans believed and were baptised into Christianity.

So runs the first sentence of an article in *West Africa* (Howard, 1989:2149). What impressed the author was the fact that the second man 'depended far less on Western missionary finance and control' than the first. The two men whose careers are being compared are Philip Quaque (1741–1816) of Ghana (then Gold Coast), the first African ordained into the priesthood of the Anglican Communion in 1765 in Exeter and London and sent to the Gold Coast as missionary and catechist in 1766, and William Wade Harris (1865–1929) of Liberia, a trail blazer and new kind of religious personage on the African scene, the first independent African Christian prophet.

In this chapter, I wish to regard Prophet Harris as a paradigm both of a non-Western and essentially *primal* apprehension of the Gospel and also of a settled self-consciousness as an African Christian uncluttered by Western missionary controls. Although Prophet Harris has not been alone in demonstrating these qualities, he exemplifies them to a very high degree. He is reported to have told a missionary who interrogated him, 'I am a prophet. Above all religion and freed from the control of men, I am under God only through the intermediary of the Angel Gabriel' (Shank, 1980:354). In his personality and career, Prophet Harris foreshadowed powerfully new insights into the Gospel emerging from the non-Western world in the changed situation of our time.

According to Harris' own account, while he was in prison in 1910 on a charge of instigating anti-government revolt, certain events changed the course of his life and made him a prophet of God and Christ. These included a trance-visitation in which the Angel Gabriel called him into the preaching ministry. In subsequent trance-visitations during his ministry,

Harris 'saw' also Moses, Elijah and Jesus: 'Moses, Angel Gabriel, Elijah, these three great prophets come and I alone speak with them' (Shank, 1980:338).· But we also know that Prophet Harris' message was quite simple: essentially based on the Bible as the Word of God, he taught that God was One and good, that people were to repent of their sins, that the cult objects of the old religion—amulets and charms—were to be destroyed, that people were to believe in Jesus, to be baptised and to join churches (he did not establish a church of his own), and that those baptised were to live a new life and to prepare for the return of Christ. In other words, Prophet Harris appeared to function in a spiritual universe which was both simple and complex, and yet which he seemed able to embrace as a totality. It is this characteristic outlook of Prophet Harris that makes him, in my view, a paradigm of 'the primal imagination'.

I should explain that I use 'primal imagination' in the same way and with the same connotation as the 1973 Consultation in Ibadan, Nigeria on Christian dialogue with traditional thought forms (within the WCC programme on Dialogue with People of Living Faiths and Ideologies) used the term 'primal world-view' (Taylor, J.B., 1976:4-5):

> It is possible ... that religious systems as such may decline, disappear from public view, or even vanish altogether, while much of the religious culture with which they have been associated may continue. In particular, many of the beliefs and values, the views about reality, man and the world, that prevailed in a primal society may survive the loss of its overt religious system and continue to provide at least part of its terms of reference in a new and more complex situation, indeed even within a new religious faith and practice. It is this structure of beliefs and values, this way of life, that may be called a primal 'world-view'.

What Harris typified we find also in another African Christian personage of our own time, Cardinal Milingo, former Roman Catholic archbishop of Lusaka, Zambia. It is quite clear from Cardinal Milingo's ministry and writings (Milingo, 1984) that he develops his theological ideas on healing, exorcism and pastoral care consciously in relation to the thought-patterns, perceptions of reality and the concepts of identity and community which prevail within the primal world-view of African societies. He does this, however, not as a mere practical convenience, but because he considers that the spiritual universe of the African primal world does offer valid perspectives for articulating Christian theological commitments.

It is important to recognise that both Harris and Milingo are deeply committed and convinced Christians. They demonstrate how the primal imagination can transcend primal religions as distinctive religious systems. It is this abiding presence of the primal world view as it occurs 'across a wide front ranging from worshippers in a continuing primal religious system to Christian believers' that I wish to convey by the use of the term 'primal imagination'. It is evident, nonetheless, that a starting-point for appreciating the primal imagination must be in primal religions themselves.

The nature of the primal world view—H.W. Turner's six-feature analysis

In 1977, Harold Turner, a sure guide into the phenomenology of the primal religions of the world, proposed a six-feature framework for understanding primal religions as authentically religious, rather than as merely epiphenomena of the social organisation of simple or pre-literate societies. Turner listed these six features as follows (Turner, 1977:30-32):

First, a sense of kinship with nature, in which animals and plants, no less than human beings, had 'their own spiritual existence and place in the universe' as interdependent parts of a whole. Accordingly, 'any object of the natural environment may enter into a totemic spiritual relationship with human beings or become tutelary and guardian spirits' whilst the environment itself is used realistically and unsentimentally but with profound respect and reverence and without exploitation. This 'ecological aspect' of primal religions, he considered to be 'a profoundly religious attitude to man's natural setting in the world'.

The *second* feature was 'the deep sense that man is finite, weak and impure or sinful and stands in need of a power not his own'. Turner linked this feature to the notion in Rudolf Otto's *The Idea of the Holy* (1950) that man's basic reaction to the Holy is in terms of a sense of creaturehood. Here too, Turner saw 'an authentic religious sensitivity, coupled with a realistic assessment of man's condition, a sensibility and an assessment that have been hidden from people like ourselves [Westerners] by the proliferation of our technical and socio-political power' (Turner, 1977:32).

The *third* feature, 'complementary to the second', was 'the conviction that man is not alone in the universe, for there is a spiritual world of powers or beings more powerful and ultimate than himself'. The universe of primal religions is thus a *personalised* universe, in which the appropriate question is not 'What caused this or that?' but '*Who* did it?' People therefore live with the awareness of the presence of transcendent powers which, however, are ambivalent. 'Not only is there the hierarchy of benevolent ancestors, and of spirits, divinities and high gods, but there is also the range of evil spirits, of demons and malevolent divinities and the lesser, more earth-born occult powers of wizards and witches'.

The *fourth* feature completes the third and is 'the belief that man can enter into relationship with the benevolent spirit-world and so share in its powers and blessings and receive protection from evil forces by these transcendent helpers'. For Turner, this feature which reveals 'the profound emphasis on the transcendent source of true life and practical salvation' goes 'contrary to all the neat projectionist theories that explain religions away' as 'man-made' and 'ignore the primary testimony of so much of the data about religions'.

The *fifth* feature, seen as an extension of the fourth, relates to the acute sense of the reality of the afterlife, a conviction which explains the important place of ancestors in many primal religions: 'In the majority of these religions, the ancestors, the "living dead" remain united in affection and in mutual obligations with the "living living"'. Indeed, the ancestors figure so prominently in the first level of the spirit world that they seem to 'create an ancestor cult and to obscure the spirit beings before whom they otherwise serve as mediators between the transcendent and the human.'

The *sixth* feature is the conviction that man lives 'in a sacramental universe where there is no sharp dichotomy between the physical and the spiritual'. Accordingly, the 'physical' acts as vehicle for 'spiritual' power, 'whilst the physical realm is held to be patterned on the model of the spiritual world beyond...' Therefore, even where there is a clear ethical dualism with respect to good and evil, nevertheless, 'one set of powers, principles and patterns runs through all things on earth and in the heavens and welds them into a unified cosmic system.'

Following this structural analysis of primal religions, Turner made several important comments. In the first place, he noted that his proposal 'may be used for the understanding of other kinds of religion besides the primal and will be found readily applicable to the Christian tradition'. Then he drew attention to a 'special relationship' of primal religions with Christianity, arising from the fact that 'in the history of the spread of the Christian faith ...its major extensions have been solely into the societies with primal religious systems'. These societies were the Mediterranean world of the early Christian centuries, and tribal peoples of Northern and Western Europe and finally the primal societies of Africa, the Pacific and parts of Asia. This meant that 'the form of religion that might seem farthest removed from the Christian [that is, from the standpoint of 19th and early 20th century Western missionary estimations of 'non-Christian religions'] has in fact had a closer relationship with it than any other.'

Therefore it came as no surprise to Turner that 'it is the people of the primal religions who have made the greatest response' to the Christian faith (Turner, 1977:37):

> There seem to be affinities between the Christian and the primal traditions, an affinity that perhaps appears in the common reactions when Christian missions first arrive ('this is what we have been waiting for') and that is further evident in the vast range of new religious movements born from the interaction between the primal religions and Christianity and in no comparable degree in the reaction of primal religions to their meeting with the other universal religions.

My own response to Turner's stimulating analysis is two-fold. In the first place, whilst affirming the six-feature structure he outlined, it is the sixth and final feature, conveying the primal conception of the universe as a unified cosmic system, essentially spiritual, that provides the real key to the entire structure. But in the second place, I am rather surprised that, having drawn attention to the special relationship of primal religions with Christianity, historical and also phenomenological, Turner saw the future for primal religions as merely 'a component within the folk religions of all cultures, or in a wider sense as part of the permanent religious heritage of all mankind'.

He did not suggest that this special relationship of primal religions with Christianity and the possibility of 'affinities' between the primal and Christian traditions could have far-reaching significance for our understanding of the nature of the Christian faith itself. For if it is the case that there is only a minimal 'paradigm-shift' as we pass from the spiritual universe of primal religions into the spiritual environment of the Christian faith ('this is what we have been waiting for'), then one would want to pursue the matter by asking how the primal imagination might bring its own 'peculiar gifts' to the shaping of Christian affirmation. The issue becomes even more pressing if Christian thought has hitherto been moulded by a world-view from which the 'living forces' of the primal imagination seem to have been expelled.

The African world and the problem of unresolved multiplicity

African Christian scholars who have examined the spiritual universe of African primal religions so far, have, to my mind, done less than full justice to the complexity of the African primal world. By stressing the centrality and uniqueness of God in African tradition, African theology has left the wider spirit-world of African primal religions—divinities, ancestors, natural forces—unaccounted for. In other words, it has answered to only part of what has been described as the 'unity and multiplicity of Divinity' (Lienhardt, 1961) in African primal religion, which I would prefer to call the unity and multiplicity of the Transcendent.

To take just two representative figures who have written extensively on the subject, Bolaji Idowu (of Nigeria) and John Mbiti (of Kenya), one gets the impression that both of these writers wish the multiplicity were not there. Because of Idowu's fundamental commitment to the vindication of an African monotheism, Idowu was definitely uncomfortable with the actual situation in Yoruba religion in which the multiplicity of divinities so 'predominate that it is difficult for the casual observer to notice that under them there is one vital cultic basis' (Idowu:1962:141). The divinities functioned as ministers of the Supreme God and Idowu was even prepared to countenance their eventual disappearance (Idowu, 1962:63).

Accordingly, the supreme service that the coming of Christianity has rendered to the Yoruba, his own people, has been to give to their 'diffused monotheism' a sharper focus and to direct attention more intently to the 'one essential Factor by which the life and belief of the Yoruba cohere and have sustenance', namely the Supreme God, Olódùmarè (Idowu, 1962:202).

John Mbiti, in his discussion of the place of divinities within the African primal universe, came to similar conclusions (Mbiti, 1969:77):

> Most, if not all, of these attributive divinities are the creation of man's imagination. This does not, however, cancel their reality: the divinities are real beings for the people concerned. With increasing scientific knowledge, no doubt, most of the divinities will be explained away and the major divinity of science will take over.

In fairness to our two eminent authors, it needs to be recognised that whilst divinities and ancestors may be found together within a particular religious structure in the African primal world, they nevertheless belong to two quite distinct categories of spiritual reality. Divinities are inherited, can be acquired and also dropped, should they prove ineffectual. Ancestors, on the other hand, being lineage personages, are irreplaceable. Consequently, in Africa, ancestors represent a more enduring problem theologically than divinities, and the intuition of Idowu and Mbiti may well be correct, that the divinities of primal religions will eventually fade away through Christian impact. Yet it has also to be pointed out that wherever this has happened in the spread of the Christian faith, it has been through a process of the demonisation of these divinities in the Christian religious consciousness. This is, in fact, the case in the more radically Christian African Independent Churches which have then re-instituted a new, Christian and biblical multiplicity, incorporating angels, Gabriel and Michael and others, with Abraham, Elijah and Jesus. The great Harris is paradigmatic of this development. If this trend is any indicator, it shows that the 'multiplicity' within the primal world-view cannot be ignored.

By establishing its link with its African world in terms of the One Supreme, Ultimate God of Africa, African theology has answered to only part of the total spiritual universe of African primal religions. What goes on in daily religious life and practice—in the company of divinities, ubiquitous spirits, ancestors—is left virtually untouched. Thus, African theology has failed to wrestle with the 'multiplicity' of the Transcendent, undercutting the contribution that it can make towards a fresh Christian account of the Transcendent, drawing on its background in the primal imagination of African religions.

Towards a fresh approach

Neither Idowu nor Mbiti fully acknowledged 'the unity and multiplicity of divinity' (or the Transcendent) in African primal religion or regarded the phenomenon as a positive element in a creative Christian engagement with the primal world view. Rather than make a reduction of divinities into attributes or manifestations of God, it may be helpful to recognise them as they are actually treated in normal religious practice, as entities which operate as ends in themselves. It could then be acknowledged that the spiritual universe of African primal religions is not without *hiatus*. It is not a neat hierarchy of divine beings and spirit-forces held in unitary harmony. The African primal world can be conceived of as a universe of distributed power, perhaps even of fragmented power; it is as much a universe of conflict as the rest of the fallen world. It is a world not of one Centre, God, but many centres, and the recognition of unity and multiplicity of the Transcendent in the African world also reveals a deep ambivalence. It is this ambivalence to which a creative Christian engagement must answer and do so in terms of the primal imagination itself.

Hitherto the mainstream of Christian theology, as a legacy of the Western philosophical approach, has tended to treat the question of the Transcendent by postulating a transcendent God. African theology too, seeking to respond to the Western interpretation (or misinterpretation) of African tradition, has fastened upon the African Transcendent God. But in 1963, John V. Taylor, himself a non-African, sought to demonstrate, in *The Primal Vision,* how little the African primal world needs a transcendent God. It is *this* life, *this* existence and its concerns, its cares, its joys which are the focus of African primal religions.

I suggest that both views were correct; only there was no dialogue between them. Most African primal religions do have a transcendent God, but the transcendent God is also part of the religious structure that yields the problem of ambivalence that was mentioned earlier. This essential point has been made by two African francophone scholars, the Rwandan philosopher, Alexis Kagame and the Congolese theologian, Mulago. In two studies on 'The place of God and man in Bantu religion', Kagame has shown that man is the centre of the universe, and, therefore, the heart of religion (Kagame, 1968, 1969); but this means man not as individual, but rather as humanity, the goal of man's centrality being the perpetuation of humankind. Kagame concluded:

> Bantu primal religion assembles its fundamental beliefs around two vital centres: God and man. The high place that God occupies is however seen as the basic presupposition which underlies the purpose of the Creator who has oriented everything towards the perpetuation of the summit of his work: humankind. (Kagame, 1969:11)

Writing on the same subject in *La religion traditionnelle des Bantus et leur vision du monde*, (1980) (a definitive work that brings together all his research on African primal religions), Mulago agreed with Kagame that Bantu religion was essentially anthropocentric. Mulago's concern, however, was to

draw out the implications for affirming a specifically African religious and
theological viewpoint (Mulago, 1980:166):

> To gain a proper understanding of African primal world-view, we must set
> aside the dualistic dialect which characterises Western thought whereby
> the exaltation of man would entail the rejection of God. On the contrary,
> African primal religious viewpoint has as its two fundamental notions and
> vital centres: God and man.

Two key ideas emerge from these studies: first, that the stress in the primal
religious world-view is decidedly *this worldly*; second, there is the notion
that this *this-worldliness* encompasses God and man in an abiding relationship with God, in other words, the divine destiny of humankind, and the
purpose and goal of the universe.

Here we need to recall the sixth and final feature in Turner's analysis,
namely, that the primal understanding discloses a universe conceived as a
unified cosmic system, essentially spiritual, in which the 'physical' acts as
sacrament for 'spiritual' power. In such a conception of the universe, the
Transcendent is not a so-called 'spiritual' world separate from the realm of
regular human existence, since human existence itself participates in the
constant interplay of the divine-human encounter. Consequently, the conclusion of Kagame and Mulago that at the heart of the universe and of religion
is a divine-human relationship for the fulfilment of humanity's divine destiny,
constitutes a real advance and lies at the heart of the contribution which
African theology, from a primal perspective, can make to a fresh Christian
account of the Transcendent. This insight signifies in Christian terms that the
revelation of God in Christ is the disclosure that God is abidingly involved in
a relationship with human beings that is intended for their good; that God
has never left them and never been far removed from them, as St. Paul declared
on Mars Hill, in Acts 17:27, in another time and place where a Christian
account of the Transcendent was being forged in an encounter with a primal
world view, the Hellenistic world-view being essentially primal. Most African
primal myths of origins being structurally anthropocentric, depict God as
departing from human company, from centre-stage, so to speak. The biblical account sharpens the ethical focus of that alienation and indicates in more
precise outline the divine commitment to reconciliation, which was already
embedded in the primal myth.

This same understanding was expressed by the Ecumenical Association
of African Theologians at Accra in 1977, speaking of an African view of the
human as an important element in African Christian theological thought
(Appiah-Kubi and Torres, 1979:193).

> For Africans there is unity and continuity between the destiny of human
> persons and the destiny of the cosmos ... The victory of life in the human

person is also the victory of life in the cosmos. The salvation of the human person in African theology is the salvation of the universe. In the mystery of the incarnation, Christ assumes the totality of the human and the totality of the cosmos.

To this whole subject John Mbiti has made a most illuminating and seminal contribution which shows a depth of primal understanding. Yet it is one which, so far as I am aware, he has never followed up (Mbiti, 1968). Recalling the five-fold categories of what he called 'African ontology' in which God, Spirits, Man, Animals, Plants and Inanimate creation exist in a 'unity, so that to break up that unity is to destroy one or more of these modes of existence, and to destroy one is in effect to destroy them all', Mbiti sought to show how the divine invasion of the world of man in the Incarnation, far from upsetting that unity, in fact retained it 'in equilibrium'. For though 'God ... in our traditional concepts lives in another mode of existence, separated from ours', He became one of us, and we can become one with Him'. The mystery of the Incarnation is, therefore, illuminated as the mystery of the mutual indwelling of God and Man in which 'no department of Man is segregated or left out'. It is no surprise that Mbiti felt confident to conclude that if the 'man of Africa' understood the Gospel in these terms, 'he will not have very far to go before he begins to walk on familiar ground'.

Therefore, the revelation of God in Christ is the revelation of transcendence. The process is not so much that of God *coming* to mankind, but rather, as the primal imagination perceives it, it is like the rending of the veil, so that the nature of the whole universe as instinct with the divine presence may be made manifest, as also the divine destiny of man as an abiding divine-human relationship. On this point, the New Testament speaks in the idiom of the primal imagination when it declares that

> Now God's home is with mankind. He will live with them, and they shall be his people. God himself will be with them, and he will be their God. (Revelation 21:3)

Even though the consummation of this divine destiny lies 'at the end', its reality in present existence must also be granted. The primal imagination is able to grasp this reality and we see evidence for it in the bold expectation with which Christian churches that are alive to their primal world-view anticipate and *do* experience 'transcendent' happenings like visions, prophecies and healings.

The community that is open to the manifestations of the Transcendent comes to participate in the Transcendent. For the Christ-event has now resulted in God's presence in space-time history in the community of his believers. Ideally, then, the Church which has come into existence through the death and resurrection of Christ, and is the household of God (1 Timothy 3:15) participates, through the Holy Spirit, in transcendence.

But is the experience of transcendence limited only to the knowledge of the love of the Father mediated through the redemptive work of the Son and actualised through the indwelling Holy Spirit? The primal imagination suggests that there is more. The clue lies in Mulago's notion of 'vital participation' as a fundamental category for understanding communal life (Mulago, 1962; 1969), in which participation in a common life and in its resources and powers constitutes community. Applied to the experience of transcendence, 'vital participation' in Christ then opens the way for a participation equally in the resources and powers of all those who also through their vital participation in Christ, are brought within the community. Since this is a community constituted in Christ and actualised through the Spirit, that is, in terms of spirit, it includes both living and dead. Thus the divine presence in the community of believers constitutes it into a 'transcendent' community in which the human components experience and share in the divine life and nature.

These are quite clearly biblical categories which are applied to Christian faith and experience, as in 1 Corinthians 10:14–22 and 2 Peter 1:4. It is interesting to find therefore, that it was this notion of 'vital participation' which David Shank, himself a non-African, used to explain how Prophet Harris came to speak of his direct involvement with Moses, Elijah, Angel Gabriel and Jesus Christ (Shank, 1980:467):

> Harris, through vital participation had been 'grafted in' to the 'holy root' of Israel's life and faith … (Romans 11:16–24). In so doing he was indeed participating in the life of the living dead and their God, of whom Jesus Himself had said, 'He is not a God of the dead but of the living, for all live unto Him' (Luke 20:33ff and parallels). Harris had earlier cut himself off from his Glebo life and family in a radical conversion; yet he was not now without living ancestors. He had simply changed family connections, now based on faith in Christ as known though Scriptures, but by means of a spirituality of vital participation totally indigenous to his African way of being.

> Prophet Harris's appropriation of the Bible as truth

> was in ways that were no longer simple patterns of 'belief in' the truth as he had known previously, but an African pattern of 'participation in' the truth. It was no longer a question of what Moses saw, or what Elijah did, or the words and works of Jesus as reported in the Bible. It became a question of involvement—as with the ancestors, the living dead—with Moses, with Elijah, with the Archangel Gabriel, and supremely with Jesus Christ.

When we are able to reformulate the Christian faith drawing on aspects of the primal imagination in the ways indicated, we can achieve a unified and organic view of the knowledge of truth, and so avoid the destructive dichotomies in epistemology which, since the European Enlightenment, have gradually drained the vital power out of Christian theology by shunting its affirmations into the siding of mere opinion. It may be necessary to recognise afresh that the real encounter with alternative viewpoints and interpretations of reality takes place not in words only, but in the realm of spirit and in things of spirit.

There may, therefore, be an even more fundamental service that the primal imagination renders to Christian theology. Modern theology in the West seems to have pursued a course of development that divorces the Christian Gospel and the issues it raises from religion and the mainsprings of human religious quests and questions. Consequently, this modern theology has lost touch with, and seems incapable of answering to, the crucial issues which lie at the heart of human existence, essentially religious issues like questions of human identity, community, ecological equilibrium and justice. Because primal world-views are fundamentally religious, the primal imagination restores to theology the crucial dimension of living religiously for which the theologian needs make no apology. The primal imagination may help us restore the ancient unity of theology and spirituality.

Perhaps a final observation on primal world views and primal religions is in order. Even though I have related my argument almost solely to evidence and literature drawn from the African field, yet primal religions cannot be adequately described as 'ethnic' religions. If in the history and phenomenology of religions, primal religions are in fact 'both primary and prior', in that they are 'the most basic or fundamental religious forms in the overall history of mankind' and 'have preceded and contributed to the other religious systems' (Turner, 1977:28), and so 'represent a common religious heritage of humanity', then the primal imagination cannot be the ethnic possession of some portions alone of the human race. The primal imagination can surface anywhere. Furthermore, if as the history of Christian expansion shows, 'it is primal religions which underlie the Christian faith of the vast majority of Christians of all ages and all nations' (Walls, 1978:11), then we need to consider the significance of 'affinities between the primal and Christian traditions'.

If Greek Orthodox Bishop AnastasiosYannoulatos, speaking at the 1973 Ibadan Conference on 'Growing into an awareness of primal world-views', out of a Christian tradition which retains perhaps the deepest feelings for Christian origins, was right in saying that a rediscovery of 'primal elements' may be what is needed (Taylor, J.B, 1976:75), this may also mean growing into a primal awareness of the Christian Gospel as religion. Primal religions generally conceive of religion as a system of power and of living religiously, as being in touch with the Source and channels of power in the universe; Christian theology in the West seems, on the whole, to understand the Christian Gospel as a system of ideas. And yet, when the apostle Paul described the Gospel, it was in terms of the Gospel as 'the power of God to save all who believe...' (Romans 1:16). Surely, this calls for a new idiom.

References

Appiah-Kubi, K & Torres, Sergio (eds.), 1979: *African Theology en route,* (New York: Orbis Books).

Howard, Kweku, 1989: 'First West African Prophet', in *West Africa*, no. 3776, (25th December 1989–7th January 1990), 2149–51.

Idowu, Bolaji, 1962: *Olódùmarè—God in Yoruba Belief,* (London: Longman).

Kagame, Alexis, 1968: 'La place de Dieu et de l'homme dans la religion des Bantu', in *Cahiers des Religions Africaines*, vol. 2, no. 4, July, (1968), 213-22;

– 1969: 'La place de Dieu et de l'homme dans la religion des Bantu', in *Cahiers des Religions Africaines*, vol. 3, no. 5; January, (1969), 5-11.

Lienhardt, G., 1961: *Divinity and Experience—the Religion of the Dinka*, (Oxford: Clarendon Press).

Mbiti, John, 1968: 'Christianity and East African culture and religion', in *Dini na Mila* (Revealed Religion and Traditional Custom), vol. 3, no. 1, May (1968).

– 1969: *African Religions and Philosophy*, (London: Heinemann).

Milingo, E., 1984: *The World in Between*, (London: C. Hurst & Co).

Mulago, gwa Cikala M., (formerly Vincent), 1962: *Un visage africain du Christianisme— L'union vital bantu face à l'unité vitale ecclésiale*, (Paris: Présence Africaine).

– 1969: 'Vital Participation', in Kwesi Dickson & Paul Ellingworth (eds.), *Biblical Revelation and African Beliefs*, (London: Lutterworth Press), 137–58.

– 1980: *La religion traditionnelle des Bantu et leur vision du monde,* (Kinshasa: Faculté de Théologie Catholique).

Otto, Rudolf, 1950: *The Idea of the Holy: An Inquiry into the Non-rational Factor in the Idea of the Divine and its Relation to the Rational* (transl. John Harvey), (London: OUP, 2nd edn).

Shank, D., 1980: *A prophet for modern times—the thought of William Wade Harris, West African precursor of the reign of Christ,*(2 vols.) PhD Thesis, Aberdeen, subsequently published as *Prophet Harris. The 'Black Elijah' of West Africa*, abridged by Jocelyn Murray, (Leiden: EJ Brill, 1994).

Taylor, John B. (ed.), 1976: *Primal World Views—Christian Involvement in Dialogue with Traditional Thought-forms*, (Ibadan: Daystar Press).

Taylor, John V., 1963: *The Primal Vision—Christian Presence amid African Religion,* (London: SCM Press).

Turner, Harold W., 1977: 'The Primal religions of the world and their study', in Victor Hayes (ed.), *Australian Essays in World Religions*, (Bedford Park: Australian Association for World Religions), 27–37.

Walls, Andrew F., 1978: 'Africa and Christian Identity', in *Mission Focus*, vol. v, no. 7, November, (1978), 11-13.

CHAPTER 8

Christian religion and African social norms: Authority, desacralisation and democracy

Introduction: Christianity's significance in African political history

[Christian] missionary education in the majority of African countries helped provide the first wave of modern African nationalists. What can all too easily be overlooked is the concurrent influences of missionary education in the direction of global awareness and the beginnings of pax humana.

This assessment of the significance of Christianity in African political history was made by one of the most authoritative African analysts of the modern political history of Africa, Ali Mazrui (1978:168). From across the continent a consistent picture emerges: even in the colonial context and in many places prior to colonialism, Christianity, through giving access to modern Western-style education, as well as through its unique message about the inalienable right to freedom of the human person, had a creative role in fostering religious and intellectual awakening that eventually led to the demise of Western political dominance. The expansion of the intellectual horizons of Africans, eased by Christianity, enhanced a new African self-understanding and self-appreciation beyond the immediate traditional circles of kinship and lineage, paving the way for the expressions of African nationalism that challenged and overturned Western rule.

As a writer more noted for his critical view of the cultural impact of Christianity upon African life, Mazrui's recognition of the religion's positive role is worth noting. He is not the only African secular historian to assign a positive role to Christianity in the modern political history of the continent. Ghanaian historian, Adu Boahen, regarded 'the spread of Christianity and Islam and especially of Western education' as an 'important social benefit of colonialism' (Boahen, 1987:104). Like Mazrui, Adu Boahen also ascribes political significance to Christianity's role in producing that universalising of African horizons, a crucial process in the transition into the expanded world that came with the Western contact. Christianity enabled Africans to participate in the European intellectual discourse and to challenge some of its assumptions; in the process, it helped produce in Africans that early political consciousness—Adu Boahen calls it 'this negative nationalism, or anticolonialism ... arising out of anger, frustration, and humiliation produced by the oppressive, discriminating and exploitative measures and activities of the colonial administrators' (Boahen, 1987: 98). Christianity's record, then, has not been one unmitigated tale of collusion with, and manipulation by, colonial administrations. As Mazrui points out, 'A distinction needs to be made between the Christian message and the European *messenger* who brought it' (Mazrui, 1978:153). Christianity has been an active participant in the struggle to regain the independence of Africa. It is the argument of this chapter that African Christianity, now with greater consciousness of its African identity and character, may face an even greater challenge to be of service to Africa in the political realm.

A new political task in Africa: from independence to democracy

Subsequently, Mazrui summarised with characteristic clarity the new political task in Africa (Mazrui, 1991: 1450):

> In the final two decades of the 20th century Africa has been undergoing ... 'the Second Liberation Struggle'. If the first liberation struggle was against alien rule, this new crusade is for African democracy. If the first liberation effort was for political independence, this second struggle is for wider human rights. If the first endeavour was for collective self-determination, this second liberation is for individual fulfilment. Africa fought hard for decolonisation in the first crusade; it remains to be seen if Africa will fight equally hard for democratisation in this second challenge.

Mazrui made this statement in his native Kenya, applying his observations to factors and forces in Kenyan political life which he saw as impediments to democratisation. He described the country as one which, in time past, was 'Africa's flagship against white minority governments' but which now 'is in danger of becoming the dragship which pulls the democratic feet behind'. Mazrui's comments drew sharp criticism from the Kenyan government which called him 'a misguided foreigner ... who does not know anything to do with his country'. Events in Kenyan political life since that exchange of views make it clear that 'the struggle for African democracy' is also the struggle for the legitimacy of dissent in African politics.

Until recently, the post-independence political histories of many African countries could be described as the process of the elimination of political dissent, that is, of organised and recognised dissent. The majority of these countries began post-colonial political life in the 1950s and early 1960s as some kind of democracy with a well-defined and recognised opposition both within and outside the legislative structures established to control national political life. By the early 1970s, these arrangements had been replaced by one-party, and in many cases military, governments. Only at the end of the 1980s did the one-party concept begin to be seriously called into question.

Yet post-colonial African politics did not lack a serious presence of alternative viewpoints. The process that led to the one-party state, in many if not all cases, involved a bitter struggle between contending interest-groups in which the winner took all and secured his gains through measures to eliminate and outlaw the loser. This process was usually justified on the grounds that indigenous African political tradition was consensual in character, so the presence of an organised opposition appearing to institutionalise the principle of adversarial politics reflected too closely the political institutions of the former colonial powers. Yet this argument often came in as a justification for actions taken on other grounds; it was not an understanding reached through sustained dialogue on the basis of a shared perspective.

My own home country, Ghana, illustrates this process. In February 1964, not quite seven years after achieving political sovereignty, the government of Ghana under the first President, Kwame Nkrumah, eliminated organised opposition and declared the country a one-party state, the flag of the ruling Convention People's Party (CPP) replacing the original national flag. The rationale for the change was that the one-party concept was 'in consonance with Ghanaian traditional political institutions which had no tradition of organised opposition and worked through a system of consultation and consensus' (Awoonor, 1990:202). This was despite the well known fact that such a consensus could not be maintained without political detentions and the removal of the right of opposition parties, *qua* opposition, to participate meaningfully in national political life. Essentially the same argument for consensual politics undergirded the careers of other political leaders in the early post-independence era: Leopold Senghor in Senegal, Julius Nyerere in Tanzania, Kenneth Kaunda in Zambia, Jomo Kenyatta in Kenya, Hastings Banda in Malawi, Sekou Toure in Guinea, Modibo Keita in Mali, and Houphouët Boigny in Côte d'Ivoire. Even in the recent quest for new democratic institutions, the same argument continues to be advanced. A sustained restatement is Kofi Awoonor's, *Ghana—A political history from pre-European to modern times* (1990). His central thesis is stated in relation to the African (extended) family understood as the basic political unit (p.9):

> Decisions of the family council are arrived at by consensus. This is the first principle in African democratic practice. In it is enshrined the notion that by consensus, all agreed on a particular line of action; opposition which could be vital for arriving at the decision therefore becomes eliminated in the aftermath of the decision being taken. Opposition as a factor in achieving consensus occurs only during deliberations. If opposition persists beyond these deliberations, then decisions are postponed until further

consultations, in order that unbending opponents of the general drift of the council's thinking can be advised and other extra parliamentary tactics employed to end the opposition. The collective and representative authority of the council is the bedrock of the consensus mode of decision-making. It emphasises the unity of the family invoking the ties that bind each member rather than drawing attention to any factors that may divide them.

Awoonor's thesis fails to solve the problem of how, within this 'consensus mode of decision-making' persons who may have responsible and legitimate grounds for dissenting from 'the general drift of the council's thinking' may express their dissent without infringing tradition. The contemporary clamour for multi-party politics in African countries constitutes an implicit challenge to the notion that political opposition, and particularly organised opposition, is somehow *un-African*. Yet the fact that political challenge as such has been discouraged in African post-colonial politics, may be a pointer to its absence in the tradition of the past. The larger question is whether, in the context of the extended pluralism of political life in modern nation-states, the traditions and political arrangements that operated in the predominantly homogeneous ethnocultural communities of the past are capable of rendering the service Awoonor seems to expect.

The religious roots of African post-independence political authoritarianism

K.A. Busia, in *Africa in search of democracy* (1967), identified this extension of scale as a major problem of political organisation in Africa. A further factor was that the traditional emphasis on solidarity, when projected on to the political institutions of the new nation-state, had an inherent tendency towards authoritarianism or the one-party state (Busia, 1967:3). But the kinship solidarity of the past was not the only element invading the present and bringing its legacy to bear upon political organisation in Africa's new nation-states. The issue of authoritarian governments in Africa in the post-independence era needs to be understood also in religious terms (Bediako, 1984:81-121), and specifically in terms of the legacy of important religious aspects of the African traditional world view as they relate to authority, power and political governance. Particularly important is the tendency of traditional society to sacralise authority and political office. The failure to recognise this has meant that a whole body of evidence has been left untouched, with the result that the era of one-party politics has been interpreted solely in 'cold-war' terms, as Africa's acceptance of the Communist prescriptions for democracy.

While such considerations have their place, they fail to take account of forces operating within African societies themselves, chief among these being religion. It is interesting that in his treatment of factors to consider in Africa's search for democracy, it was what he called 'the religious heritage' that Busia placed first (Busia, 1967:1f). Curiously, however, though Busia had seen so clearly the pervasive influence of religion in traditional political life, he appeared not to have recognised that the sacralisation of power in traditional society would have any significance for understanding Africa's new problems in politics, nor affect the new search for democracy. In *African Political Systems* (1940; 1987), anthropologists Meyer Fortes and Evans-Pritchard drew attention to this factor in traditional politics (p.16):

> An African ruler is not to his people merely a person who can enforce his will on them. He is the axis of their political relations, the symbol of their unity and exclusiveness and the embodiment of their essential values. He is more than a secular ruler ... His credentials are mystical and are derived from antiquity.

The explanation for the 'mystical credentials' of the African ruler is the crucial political role of ancestors in virtually all African societies, both those with centralised authority and those that lack it. Since the traditional belief is that the well-being of the society depends upon maintaining good relations with the ancestors on whom the living depend for help and protection, the ruler fulfils an important function as intermediary, and is the central figure at the instituted religious rituals ensuring the maintenance of the desired harmony between the living and the ancestors. Thus, the authority of the ruler in the traditional political system is the authority of the ancestors. In the usage of the Akans (of Ghana), for example, the traditional ruler is 'the one who sits on the stool of the ancestors' (Busia, 1968: 36f).

This crucial role of ancestors in traditional political organisation means that as well as the office of the ruler, the whole realm of politics is sacralised, since the traditional world-view makes no sharp dichotomy between 'secular' and 'sacred' realms of existence. In the traditional perspective too, the concept of the state is inclusive of the living and the ancestors, so that institutions of political and social organisation acquire a sacral character through their association with ancestors. As Fortes and Evans-Pritchard observed (1989:18), 'The social system is, as it were, removed to a mystical plane, where it figures as a system of sacred values beyond criticism or revision'.

By thus reckoning the authority of living rulers to be that of ancestors, African tradition appeared to make every challenge to political authority an attack upon the sacral authority of ancestors on whose goodwill and favour the community's continuance and prosperity are held to depend. Any radical political challenge would seem to suggest the subversion of tradition and custom and indeed, of the very foundations of the identity and continuity of the state or community itself. Thus, by functioning as the guarantor of the authority of living rulers, the ancestor cult becomes the most potent symbol of the sacralisation of authority and power in African traditional politics.

It is my view that the problems of African post-independence politics are not unrelated to these aspects of African traditional politics (Bediako, 1984). The sacralisation of authority and political power found its way into the new political ideologies and experiments embarked upon in the new nation-states, though as 'secular' parodies, lacking the kinds of checks and balances of the old religious universe of meaning. The ready justification of the one-party concept, the precarious fortunes of political dissent and the tenacity with which unpopular rulers continued to cling to power, all suggest that in the politics of independent Africa, one was still encountering the 'old' ancestor who never ceases to reign from the realm of spirit-power. The honorific titles and praise-names of some African heads of state convey ancestral overtones. When President Nkrumah adopted the title 'Osagyefo', portraying himself as 'Saviour' and 'Redeemer', he was not promoting the interests of the old traditional rulers. Instead the title portrayed him as 'Saviour' and 'Redeemer' from the misfortunes of colonialism, and virtually as the eponymous ancestor-founder of the nation. Ghana's coins bore his image, with the inscription: 'Civitatis Ghaniensis Conditor'(Founder of the Ghanaian State). President Nkrumah, for all practical purposes, became an ancestor-ruler in the old sacral sense. As John Pobee has shown (1988:146), the President even 'approved of being accorded a supernatural status'. This persistence of the sacralisation of power in the era of post-independence politics occurred in several African countries.

For African nations caught between their legacy of the one-party concept and the perceived need for change in the direction of a genuine democratic pluralism, the challenge is not to 'run a democracy' by the mere adoption of the external trappings of democratic reform. If African politics in the future is to be able to integrate a wider political pluralism and to manifest a greater tolerance of dissent, that is, exhibit fundamental assumptions of genuine democratic culture, then African societies need to put in place new conceptions of political authority and power. I am persuaded that in this connection, African Christianity may have some distinctive contributions to offer.

Christianity and the de-sacralisation of authority and power in history

By the close association of religious (sacred) authority and political power in the person of the traditional ruler, African traditional societies were 'ontocracies', sacralising authority and power with the effectual integration of altar and throne (van Leeuwen, 1964:165ff). Historically, Christianity has been a de-sacralising force. A comparison of the institution of kingship of ancient Egypt and Babylon with the monarchy in ancient Israel, provides illuminating examples of the impact that Hebrew prophetic religion was intended to have on conceptions of authority and the exercise of power in human society.

Indeed, to the Hebrew prophets, *all* rulers—be they the sacral rulers of Egypt and Babylon, or the unsacral kings of Israel—are mere mortals among fellow mortals, and can be summoned to account before God. To the kingdoms of the world there is an alternative and overarching kingdom, the Kingdom of God, to which the kingdoms of the world must bow and submit. It was the quality of her faith that kept ancient Israel from going the way of her neighbours (Frankfort:1948).

The essential thrust of the New Testament is the continuation of this desacralising impact. Undoubtedly, Jesus' message about the Kingdom of God was not perceived as other-worldly or as politically neutral by the authorities of his day. They saw him as a threat and a challenge, and had him executed as a political criminal: 'We caught this man misleading our people, telling them not to pay taxes to the Emperor, and claiming that he himself is the Messiah, a king', his accusers said to Pilate (Luke 23:2). Similarly, when Jesus said to Pilate, 'My kingdom is not of this world' (John 18:36), he could not have meant that it had nothing to do with the world, for if he had, then at a most crucial point in his career, the fundamental commitment of the mission of Jesus to human history and its transformation, signified in the doctrine of the Incarnation, breaks down. His meaning could only have been that he held a conception of authority, that is, power in the political sense, which was essentially 'other' than that which Pilate held. Pilate's claim to have 'power either to free or to crucify' Jesus is the indication that his conception of power sacralised the political authority of the Empire. It points to the failure of all sacralisation to recognise the essentially derivative character of all earthly power. On the other hand, Jesus' response: 'You would have no power over me if it were not given to you from above' represents Jesus' de-sacralisation of the Empire itself. Pilate's authority, as that of the earthly Empire, 'like all human authority, is *delegated*; its source is Divine and therefore it is not arbitrary power, which can be exercised capriciously without moral blame' (Bernard, 1928:619).

Fundamentally, authority belongs to, and derives from, the transcendent realm. Here Christian teaching affirms African tradition: authority, political power, does not reside with human beings, nor even with the sacral ruler, for is he not merely 'the one who sits on the stool of the ancestors'? But Christianity would take the argument further. For if authority does not reside with the merely human, then why should it be located in the realm of the essentially *human* spirits of the ancestors? In Christian perspective, ancestors too become de-sacralised. Authority truly belongs only to God. Pilate's unease or fear (John 19:8) in the presence of Jesus indicates that Pilate, in his attempt to exert his authority by ascribing 'to himself almost the divine prerogative which is actually true of Jesus', only discovers that 'he is confronted with one who is himself at the source of all authority. The tables are turned and Pilate is judged by the one whom he judges' (Lindars, 1972:568).

The way of Jesus revealed a new political option in the world of his time. His was not the way of the Sadducees and Herodians, preserving their religion through pragmatism and expediency by collaborating with the Roman occupying forces. His was not the way of the Zealots, the violent revolutionaries out to overturn Roman rule by force. Nor was it the way of the Essenes who chose withdrawal into the desert so as to preserve their religious life intact, nor of the Pharisees who preoccupied themselves with their religious observances and segregated themselves politically. Jesus' way was one of engagement and involvement through a new way of overcoming, arising from a unique concept of power—the power of forgiveness over retaliation, of suffering over violence, of love over hostility, of humble service over domination. Jesus won his way to pre-eminence and glory, not by exalting himself, but by humbling himself, to the point of dying a shameful death. In other words, his conception of power was that of non-dominating power. By making himself of no account, everyone must now take account of him (Philippians 2:10-11) (Yoder, 1971:13-33).

Thus, the ultimate clue to what Jesus meant in his words to Pilate, as well as the logic of his own mind on the question of authority and power, are conveyed by his Cross, the means of his death which Pilate sanctioned and Jesus willingly embraced. By his Cross, Jesus de-sacralised all worldly power, relativising its inherent tendency in a fallen universe to absolutise itself. But the Cross de-sacralises *all* the powers, institutions and structures that rule human existence and history—family, nation, social class, race, law, politics, economy, religion, culture, tradition, custom, ancestors—stripping them of any pretensions to ultimacy. This 'concrete social meaning of the Cross' (Yoder, 1972:134), illuminates Paul's terminology of 'principalities', 'powers', 'thrones', 'dominions', and their cognate expressions, which, far from being the elements of a mythological outlook, have been shown (Berkhof, 1962; Yoder, 1972; Wink, 1984; 1986; 1992), to be relevant to the conditions of modern existence. In the African setting, it is through an African reading of the Scriptures, particularly in African languages, and by paying attention to the resonances of the biblical categories into the African primal world-view, that the desacralising impact of the Gospel is experienced afresh. Since the roots of sacralisation in African tradition lie in *religion*, it is in terms of *religion* that it can be adequately encountered. It is as *religion* that the Christian Gospel is able to meet the African world in depth. The primal world-view conceives of religion as power; the Gospel is the power of God (Romans 1:16). However, 'if Christianity desacralises, it does not de-spiritualise. The African world continues a spiritual world; what changes is the configuration of forces. The human environment remains the same, but the answers to its puzzles are different' (Bediako, 1987:456).

In the present quest for new political arrangements in Africa, the discussion is often distorted, so that it seems as if the choice is between 'Western' forms of political organisation and 'indigenous' African systems and patterns. That distinction may sometimes be valid. It is important to realise, however, that so-called Western democracy is not inherently indigenous to the Western world, nor is it exclusively the preserve of the West, for it has emerged largely under the impact of Christian political ideas. But because many Western nations, under the impact of secularisation, have lost touch with the Christian roots of their political institutions, it is not sufficiently realised that Christianity has, in fact, played a key role in the emergence of freedom in the modern world. One result of this inadequate appreciation of the role of Christian religion in the world, is that in Africa in particular, political theorists, historians and governments have continued to nurse a suspicion of Christianity as somehow alien, alienating and unhelpful in dealing with the modern questions of African political and cultural identity.

A proper understanding of the issues shows that the struggle for true democracy in Africa involves making room for the 'way of Jesus', the way of non-dominating power, in the political arrangements under which members of society and nation relate to one another. The mind of Jesus on the questions of politics and power is *not* a dominating mind, *not* a self-pleasing or self-asserting mind, but a saving mind, a redemptive mind, a servant mind. 'For Christ did not please himself' (Romans 15:3). Jesus' way of dealing with political power represents the perfect desacralisation of all worldly power. The recognition that power truly belongs to God, rooted in the Christian theology of power as non-dominating, liberates politicians and rulers to be humans among fellow humans, and ennobles politics and the business of government into the business of God and the service of God in the service of fellow humans. This perspective provides the only genuine and abiding foundation for any serious quest in Africa for a sustained culture of freedom and justice in a genuine democracy. 'Without such a conception of power as Jesus held, taught, and demonstrated by the Cross, the hope of achieving a real sharing of political power ... will remain elusive' (Bediako, 1990:29).

What are the indications that Christian Africa will be able to rise to this challenge in coming decades? In 1969 Harold Turner published an article, 'The place of independent religious movements in the modernisation of Africa' (Turner, 1969:43-63), in which he countered the view that these movements, mainly the new Independent churches of Africa, were ignorant and reactionary, compensating people for a miserable life in a turbulent Africa by diverting energies from national development and modernisation. He showed, on the contrary, that these movements had made a significant contribution to the rise of modern African nationalism, to the transcendence of ethnic allegiances, and to areas of positive social and economic transformation. They had contributed to the de-sacralisation of political life by avoiding, on the whole, becoming the spiritual arm of the new nationalisms.

The Christian churches of Africa live in contexts of relative material poverty, amid some of the most vulnerable economies in the world at the present time. As the churches have registered growth in membership, so have the burdens grown which they have had to carry to sustain their witness and ministries. But the increasing social and economic hardships have also been accompanied by a deepening of Christian consciousness, especially in relation to various pressing national issues and the need to be relevant to questions at the grassroots of society. This means that, when the need has arisen, the churches, on the whole, have not been ill-prepared.

The subject of this chapter has been the desacralisation of political power in African society and the contribution Christianity can make to this process. The evidence that this is already happening can be found in the careers of Archbishop Desmond Tutu and other church leaders in South Africa in the struggle against the white ontocracy of apartheid, of church leaders in Kenya in the struggle for democratic pluralism and open government, in the united stance of the Christian Council of Ghana and the Catholic Bishops' Conference against the curtailing of human rights in Ghana, to cite just a few instances. As country after country has embarked upon the path of democratic pluralism, the Christian churches, their bishops, moderators and other leaders, have been called upon to stand in the breach to act as interim chairmen and presidents of numerous negotiations and national conferences held to smooth the way into the new political dispensation. It is as if the embarrassment of the colonial connection, real or imaginary, that was Christianity's burden in the immediate post-independence era, has been effectively lived down. The Christian churches are now recognised as institutions with genuine commitment to African concerns and with a deep understanding of African problems from an African perspective, arising out of their Christian convictions.

But Africa has not produced and is not likely to produce, a new Christendom. The Christian autocracy in Ethiopia and the white Christian autocracy in South Africa have gone. All Christian churches in Africa exist in contexts of religious pluralism and will have to continue learning to worship God and his Christ, witness to the Gospel, survive in joy, and strive for peace and justice and democratic freedom for all. Christian evangelisation and nurture, and hence the Church, are essential elements in the process whereby a society's outlook, value-systems, thought-patterns and social and political arrangements become permeated with the mind of Jesus. As the first-fruits of the new humanity, created through the reconciling—by the Cross—of hostile groups (Ephesians 2:14), the Church must manifest the victory of the Cross in the concrete realities of her existence in society, and demonstrate that she has begun to be liberated from bondage to the 'powers' that rule human existence and the cosmic order in that context. Christian conversion and Christian conviction need to find concrete expression in relation to the 'elemental forces'—ethnicity, race, social class, culture and customs—that shaped individual and social identity and destiny in the old order.

The major challenge now facing the Christian churches in Africa in the political sphere is to raise to consciousness in the wider society the connection between the Church's message of righteousness, love and justice, and the search for sustainable democratic governance, though the churches must continually remember that the search for democracy is not an end in itself. As the end of human existence is the biblical vision of *shalom* in the Kingdom of God, the arrival of democracy is not the coming of the Kingdom.

References

Awoonor, Kofi, 1990: *Ghana—A political history from pre-European to modern times,* (Accra: Sedco).

Bediako, Kwame, 1984: 'Biblical Christologies in the context of African Traditional Religions', in Vinay Samuel & Chris Sugden (eds.), *Sharing Jesus in the Two-Thirds World,* (Grand Rapids: Eerdmans), 81-121.

– 1987: 'Christ in Africa—Some reflections on the contribution of Christianity to the African Becoming', in Christopher Fyfe (ed.), *African Futures* (Proceedings of a conference held in the Centre of African Studies, University of Edinburgh, 9-11 December, 1987), (Edinburgh: Centre of African Studies).

– 1990: *Jesus in African Culture—A Ghanaian perspective,* (Accra: Asempa Publishers).

Berkhof, Hendrik, 1962: *Christ and the Powers,* (Scottdale: Herald Press).

Bernard, J.H., 1928: *The Gospel according to St John* (The International Critical Commentary, 2 vols.), (Edinburgh: T. & T. Clark).

Boahen, Adu, 1987: *African Perspectives on Colonialism,* (Baltimore: Johns Hopkins University Press).

Busia, K.A., 1967: *Africa in Search of Democracy,* (London: Routledge & Kegan Paul).

– 1968: *The position of the Chief in the modern political system of Ashanti—A study of the influence of contemporary social changes on Ashanti political institutions,* (London: Frank Cass; first published in 1951).

Fortes, M. & Evans-Pritchard, E.E. (eds.),1987: *African Political Systems,* (London: KPI (in association with the International African Institute); first published in 1940).

Frankfort, H., 1948: *Kingship and the Gods—A study of Ancient Near Eastern Religion as the integration of Society and Nature,* (Chicago: The University of Chicago Press).

Leeuwen, Arend Th. van, 1964: *Christianity in World History: The meeting of the Faiths of East and West,* (ET by H.H. Hoskins), (London: Edinburgh House Press).

Lindars, Barnabas, 1972: *The Gospel of John* (New Century Bible), (London: Oliphants).

Mazrui, A., 1978: *Political Values and the Educated Class in Africa,* (London: Heinemann).

– 1991: in *West Africa,* 2–8 September, 1450.

Pobee, John, 1988: *Kwame Nkrumah and the Church in Ghana: 1949-1966—A study in the relationship between the socialist government of Kwame Nkrumah, the first Prime Minister and first President of Ghana, and the Protestant Christian Churches in Ghana,* (Accra: Asempa Publishers).

Turner, Harold, 1969: 'The place of independent religious movements in the modernisation of Africa' in *Journal of Religion in Africa,* vol. 2, fasc. 1, (1969), 43–63.

Yoder, J.H., 1971: *The Original Revolution—Essays on Christian Pacifism,* (Scottdale: Herald Press).

– 1972: *The Politics of Jesus,* (Grand Rapids: Eerdmans).

Wink, Walter, 1984: *Naming the Powers—The Language of power in the New Testament,* (Minneapolis: Fortress Press).

– 1986: *Unmasking the Powers—The invisible forces that determine human existence,* (Minneapolis: Fortress Press).

– 1992: *Engaging the Powers—Discernment and resistance in a world of domination,* (Minneapolis: Fortress Press).

CHAPTER 9

Towards a new understanding of Christian history in the post-missionary era

Introduction: the new global impact of the Third World Church

In 1971, American Jesuit scholar, John Schumacher, working in theological education teaching history in the Philippines, published an article under the title: 'The Third World and the Twentieth Century Church'. In it he related the emergent Third World Church to the study of Christian history in view of the changed situation of world Christianity, seeking to establish fundamentally one point, that

> The entrance into the full life of the Church of the peoples of the Third World, acutely conscious of their aspirations to national development and self-realisation, has had a manifold effect on the whole Church's self-understanding. (Schumacher, 1974:207)

Schumacher identified four areas in which the principle elements in the new self-understanding are due primarily to the Third World, or Two-Thirds World, as we would say. The *first* was the realisation of an essential cultural plurality in unity belonging within the universal Church; no longer would it be taken for granted that the manifestations of Christian presence would merely replicate patterns and forms in the West. *Second*, there was a new attitude to the values of non-Christian religions, and a new perception of the Church's relation to them. In Schumacher's view, it is the impact of the Third World that has compelled the twentieth century Church to look at non-Christian religions, not merely to understand them, but also to 'find in them true religious values which perhaps have been obscured in the Western Christian presentation or formulation of God's Word to man'. The *third* area of influence from the Third World upon the universal Church has been to bring about a broader understanding of the role of the Church as witness to the Word of God, causing the Church to adopt a humbler, servant posture among the peoples it encounters, rather than the stance of crusader or inquisitor. The *fourth* area of the Third World's impact was 'a fuller concept of the mission of the Church as embracing not only the ministry of the Word and sacraments but active involvement in economic and all human development' and the struggle for justice in the world. For Schumacher, the Christian life of the churches of the Third World constituted an important theological factor for Christian scholarship and so belonged, not on the margin, but in the mainstream of Christian history.

Yet, according to Schumacher, Christian scholarship and ecclesiastical historiography in particular, were continuing to ignore the weight and significance of Third World churches, treating them 'more as manifestations of the Christian life of the church which evangelised them than as new incarnations of the Church in cultures having their own contribution to make to the fullness of the people of God' (Schumacher, 1974:212). What was required to correct this was for ecclesiastical historiography not only to become 'conscious of the new centre of gravity of the people of God' but also to show how the history of the people of God in the nations of the Third World forms 'an integral part of the continuation of the history of salvation into which the younger churches have been inserted in God's due time, as the Gospel came from Jerusalem through Greece and Rome to Europe, and to the Third World through Europe.' Within this understanding of ecclesiastical historiography, 'it is surely far more important to know the progress of Christian life during a single century among one entire people of the Third World than to investigate the *minutiae* of the history of any number of medieval European monasteries, long since extinct', unless the Church historian is to be 'merely an ecclesiastical antiquarian'.

In the same period, a similar questioning of the trend of Christian scholarship was expressed by the Kenyan Anglican theologian, John Mbiti, at the time Director of the World Council of Churches Ecumenical Institute, Bossey, in Switzerland (Mbiti, 1976). Mbiti called attention to the danger of the Church becoming 'kerygmatically universal', while remaining 'theologically provincial'. As 'the axis of Christendom appeared to shift from the Northern to the Southern regions of the world' so that 'the centres of the Church's universality were no longer in Geneva, Rome, Athens, Paris, London, New York, but Kinshasa, Buenos Aires, Addis Ababa and Manilla', there did not seem to be a corresponding shift toward 'mutuality and reciprocity in the theological task facing the universal Church'. The problem was in a one-sidedness in theological learning in the Church (Mbiti, 1976:16-17):

> Theologians from the new (or younger) churches have made their pilgrimages to the theological learning of the older churches. We had no alternative. We have eaten theology with you; we have drunk theology with you; we have dreamed theology with you. But it has all been one-sided; it has all been, in a sense, your theology … We know you theologically. The question is do you know us theologically? Would you like to know us theologically?

As a result of this absence of mutuality and reciprocity in theological learning in the Church, Mbiti saw that there was 'a real and yet false dichotomy at the heart of the Church's very experience of universality. This dichotomy is real because it is there; it is false because it ought not to be there'. One indicator of the lopsidedness in the Church's experience of universality and therefore a false universality, was the fact that the theology that was brought from the pilgrimage to the theological learning in the older churches seemed unable to cope with the new concerns in the new churches. To illustrate his point, Mbiti told a story (Mbiti, 1976:6-8):

> He learned German, French, Greek, Latin, Hebrew, in addition to English, church history, systematics, homiletics, exegesis and pastoralia, as one part of the requirements for his degree. The other part, the dissertation, he wrote on some obscure theologian of the Middle Ages. Finally he got what he wanted: a Doctorate in Theology. It took him nine and a half years altogether, from the time he left his home until he passed his orals and set off to return. He was anxious to reach home as soon as possible, so he flew, and he was glad to pay for his excess baggage which, after all, consisted only of the Bible in various languages he had learned, plus Bultmann, Barth, Bonhoeffer, Brunner, Buber, Cone, Küng, Moltmann, Niebuhr, Tillich, Christianity Today, Time Magazine. ... At home relatives, neighbours, old friends...all gather to welcome him back. ... Dancing, jubilation, eating, feasting—all these go on as if there were nothing else to do, because the man for whom everyone had waited has finally returned. ... Suddenly there is a shriek. Someone has fallen to the ground. It is his older sister ...he rushes to her. People make room for him and watch him. 'Let's take her to the hospital,' he calls urgently. They are stunned. He becomes quiet. They all look at him bending over her. Why doesn't someone respond to his advice? Finally a schoolboy says, 'Sir, the nearest hospital is 50 miles away, and there are few buses that go there.' Someone else says, 'She is possessed. Hospitals will not cure her!' The Chief says to him, 'You have been studying theology overseas for 10 years. Now help your sister. She is troubled by the spirit of her great aunt.' He looks around. Slowly he goes to get Bultmann, looks at the index, finds what he wants, reads again about spirit possession in the New Testament. Of course he gets the answer: Bultmann has demythologised it. He insists that his sister is not possessed. The people shout, 'Help your sister, she is possessed!' He shouts back, 'But Bultmann has demythologised demon possession.'... Fantasy? No, for these are the realities of our time.

Mbiti added that the story was entirely fictional and not based on the experience of a real person. In order to overcome the false universality which produced this 'theological impotence', the Church in the North and the Church in the South should 'embrace each other's concerns and stretch to each others horizons'. This was all the more important as the axis of Christianity tilted southwards 'towards areas, situations, cultures, concerns, traditions, religions and problems which are largely different from those which have precipitated or necessitated the theological output of the Church in the West over the last 500 years at least' (Mbiti, 1976:10).

It is important to understand the grounds upon which Mbiti made these observations: it was essential to recognise the theological significance of the concerns of the Church in the South not merely for the sake of the South; rather 'only in that way can the universality of the Church be meaningful both evangelistically and theologically' (Mbiti, 1976:9). To speak of the southward shift of Christianity does not mean that the South alone now matters theologically. Rather, what must be stressed is that the southward shift of the church's axis has given Christianity what John Mbiti called new 'centres of universality'and raises important questions about theology and Christian identity as the church becomes truly universal for the first time in its history. Christianity is indeed entering upon a new intellectual phase, with a new and unique sense of its universality. In his survey of 'The Christian tradition in Today's World' (Walls, 1987), Andrew Walls traces the process of this effectual universal diffusion of Christianity to a considerably earlier period, seeing 'a culmination and acceleration' since 1945, since the start of the era of decolonisation. The convergence of the two processes has been decisive since it has meant that the new and unique sense of Christianity's universality has also been, in effect, the 'decolonisation' of Christianity. For obvious reasons it has been in the recently decolonised parts of the world, the new centres of Christianity's universality. that this new Christian intellectual climate has been felt most intensely. The meaning of this new reality for understanding the nature of Christian history and, therefore, of Christian missionary theology in our post-missionary era, will be explored in the remainder of this chapter.

Theologies of the South: a new way of doing theology

These developments in Christianity have come to maturity since the 1970s and 1980s when one began to speak of 'Third World theology' or 'Theologies of the Third World' as a distinct element within the broad field of Christian scholarship, distinguishable from the Western or European tradition. Constraints prohibit a detailed analysis of the theologies of the South. What is important is to understand the general direction and broad trends, and to appreciate those characteristics that the emergent theologies from the new centres of Christianity's universality have in common.

It would be an exaggeration to say that the emergence of the theological activity of the South has involved a complete break with the tradition of the West. Latin American Liberation Theology, for instance, owed a lot to the political theology associated with the work of German Reformed theologian, Jürgen Moltmann, as well as to some areas of French Roman Catholic thought in the 20th century. But these theologians were themselves open to the Third World. Yet in important respects, theological activity as specifically Christian activity, has undergone radical transformations in the new centres, particularly in relation to mission. All expressions of contextual theology in the South are essentially missionary theologies, arising out of efforts to let the Gospel encounter the reality of the South in all its complexities.

It is important also to understand how, in the minds of the promoters themselves, this new theological activity becomes closely linked with meetings, conferences and associations, even when they have already embarked upon a career of theological writing. It is usual, for instance, to take Gustavo Guttierrez's *A Theology of Liberation* (1973) as the literary inauguration of Latin American Liberation Theology. Latin American Liberation Theology, as a theology from the South, as theology 'from the periphery', belongs, however, within the movement that was effectually only launched with the formation of the Ecumenical Association of Third World Theologians in 1976, when 22 theologians from Latin America, Asia, Africa, the Caribbean and Black America met at Dar-es-Salaam in Tanzania. According to Sergio Torres (from Chile), the first Executive Secretary (Torres, 1988):

> The first major achievement of Dar-es-Salaam was to create a new space for self-expression ... the Third World theologians were separated and without any forum of common communication. The Dar-es-Salaam dialogue allowed them to meet and to establish together a space or permanent forum where their humiliated and suffering voice could be heard, with the hope that God would hear this people...

This could equally be said of the first Conference in March 1982, in Bangkok, Thailand, on the theme of Christology, which launched the International Fellowship of Evangelical Mission Theologians from the Two-Thirds World, comprising the Latin American Theological Fraternity, Partnership In Mission-Asia and the African Theological Fraternity (now Fellowship). The editors of the Conference Proceedings defined the conference's own self-understanding (Samuel and Sugden, 1984:viii):

> The Conference was ... a creative workshop to facilitate and promote reflection in community. It was a meeting and a fellowship of persons, testing and affirming insights gained from diverse cultural and theological backgrounds to deepen their understandings of Christ. ... the product of the Conference was thus more than a collection of papers. It was the creation, experience and development of community.

This leads us to the single most important observation on the transformation of theological activity in the new centres. Whilst individual promoters have continued their literary output under their own names, the theological activity itself is seen as a shared activity emerging out of a shared experience. The 'testing and affirming of insights' takes place in the context of a shared 'space', in 'the experience and development of community'. But here community is understood as embracing more than the circle of scholars. The explicit claim is that this is the 'theology of the people'. In the words of the late Engelbert Mveng of Cameroon (former Executive Secretary of the Ecumenical Association of African Theologians), on African Theology (this would apply especially to South African Black Theology):

> It expresses the faith and hope of our oppressed peoples. It illustrates the experience of the living Christian communities in Africa. It is therefore not an academic theology even if some of its promoters move in university circles. (Mveng, 1988:18)

On the question of the linguistic medium of this theological activity, Mveng continues:

> When the objection is made that this theology is not written in native languages, we reply that it is lived in native languages, in the villages and in the neighbourhoods, before being translated into foreign languages by its own rightful heirs, the African theologians.

Perhaps even more than in African Theology, it is in Latin American Liberation Theology that theological activity as the experience of community and as 'theology of the people' has been most forcefully exploited. In the words of Brazilian theologian, Leonardo Boff (1988:13):

> Liberation theology has defined another place in which theology is 'done': not so much the university or institute and more the community and in service to the community ... Those who do this theology are not so much individual theologians as the communities who bring their problems, solutions, actions and thinking to be taken up and worked on by theologians.

Boff's own literary career cannot be adequately understood apart from his close association with the 'grassroots ecclesial communities' of which he became 'national adviser'. The whole rationale of the Minjung Theology from South Korea is captured in the name: 'Minjung', that is, 'people', ordinary people as the subjects of history and theology. This conception of theology as fundamentally the experience of community underlies what the conference in Dar-es-Salaam felt to be the 'most novel aspect' of the emergent theologies from the South, and which led the participants to speak in their Final Statement of an epistemological break with traditional academic theology as they knew it in the West (Torres & Fabella, 1988:269):

> We reject as irrelevant an academic type of theology that is divorced from action. We are prepared for a radical break in epistemology which makes commitment the first act of theology and engages in critical reflection on the praxis of the reality of the Third World.

This 'first act' of commitment to 'the praxis of the reality of the Third World' is essentially a commitment to liberation in all its dimensions, spiritual as well as socio-political, individual as well as collective and cosmic. Here 'Liberation' becomes synonymous with 'theology', or rather theological activity. It is the idea, in the words of the Indian theologian, Samuel Rayan, that in theology, 'truth is not something that can be known and spoken independently of its realisation in life'. In the Third World reality of 'poverty, powerlessness and religious pluralism', such a commitment ties theological activity inextricably into the service of liberation.

This commitment led also to the realisation that such theological activity needed a spirituality, that 'a theology seeking to be of service to the people must necessarily be a theology that starts with a meeting with God, a meeting that takes place within a situation of challenge, a situation that awakens Christians to a contemplative commitment' (Rayan, 1978:119). Some, like Engelbert Mveng, have spoken of this spirituality of liberation as the spirituality of the Beatitudes of the Gospels, 'not as the eschatological result of liberation, but rather its theological foundation' (Mveng, 1978:19). In other words, it is from the standpoint of the liberation of the Kingdom of God that theological activity can confront the 'other kingdom' which 'breeds poverty, destitution, injustice, tears, hard-heartedness, iniquity, discord and war, intolerance and persecution'. For Mveng, this quality of the spirituality of liberation makes the theology of liberation itself of universal relevance.

I wish to stress that the conception of theology as born of community and spiritual experience has helped to restore to the theologies of the South, at least in their intellectual frame of reference and methodology, the unity of theology and spirituality. This, no doubt, has been helped by the massive presence of religion on these continents and by the fact that the Christian churches have been experiencing growth and religious awakening. As a consequence, a so-called 'secular theology' or the transformation of theology into a social ethic, has so far been avoided. Even Latin America Liberation theologians who at the start were much less interested in the question of religion in its own terms because of their inclination towards Marxian categories of social analysis, soon came to recognise that their reality also includes a 'popular religiosity' which is a religious phenomenon to be taken seriously. Some years after *A Theology of Liberation,* Gustavo Guttierez was to write a different kind of book, *We drink from our own wells* (1983). Accordingly, the theologies of the South seem to have been able to affirm with much greater confidence that not only is theology born of spirituality, but also, in its Christian specificity, is born of faith in Jesus Christ and the following of Jesus in the perspective of liberation. Thus, Sri Lankan Jesuit theologian, Aloysius Pieris, has written:

> Spirituality is not the practical conclusion of theology but the radical involvement with the poor and the oppressed, and is what creates theology. We know Jesus the truth by following Jesus the way. (Pieris, 1988:82)

Because of the strong element of 'the experience of community' in the theologies of the South, these theologies have a distinct inclination to being 'ecclesial' theologies, which is not to say that they are confessional or denominational. This simply expresses the way in which the theologies of the South are rooted in the churches and produced from within the churches, to the extent that they proceed by seeking to understand and articulate the longings and aspirations of the communities they represent. This same inclination has tended to make the theologies of the South ecumenical, with a concern to be Christian and true to context—Asian or Latin American, or African, rather than simply Catholic, or Lutheran or Reformed. Theologians of the South are hardly found discussing or defending the Catholic or the Protestant view of a particular doctrine for its own sake. When Allan Boesak wished to affirm his identification with the Reformed tradition in the history of Christianity, it was to say he was 'Black and Reformed' (Boesak, 1984).

This characteristic of the theologies of the South points to one of the profoundest criticisms of Western theology made by the theologians of the South, that Western theology was for so long presented in all its particulars as *the* theology of the Church, when, in fact, it was geographically localised and culturally limited, European and Western, and not universal. The southward shift of the Church, with the growth and vitality of the Christian communities of the South has changed all that. Some theologians of the South speak of this phenomenon as 'the displacement of theology from the centre to the periphery' and would like to ascribe a particular form of universality to the new theological methodology from the South, on the basis that it is *a new way* of doing theology, the way of liberation. This is simply a plea to be taken seriously, the affirmation of the space that is needed for authentic expression.

Christian History: its new shape

I too wish to argue that the church's learning experience in the South has a universal relevance, but I understand that relevance differently and I intend to arrive at my conclusion by a different route, by discussing what this southward shift of the Church means for our understanding of the nature of Christian history.

In the first place, rather than speak of a 'displacement from centre to periphery' I would say with John Mbiti, that the southward shift of the Church has caused to emerge 'new centres of Christianity's universality'. Wherever the faith has been transmitted and assimilated are equally 'centres of Christianity's universality'. This is not to deny that there have been (and the modern Western world is not the first of these) instances of Christian recession. What is important is that a shift in the centre of gravity of Christianity is precisely that: a shift in the centre of gravity of *Christianity*. It points more to the nature of the faith and less to the significance of the human agencies of its transmission. Absolutisation of the pattern of Christianity's transmission should consequently be avoided and the nature of Christian history itself be re-examined. We are constantly in danger of re-inventing the Deuteronomic law of the single sanctuary (Deuteronomy 12) and of requiring, in the old language of the Western Church, that *ubi ecclesia ibi Christus*, (where the Church is, there is Christ). Yet the deeper biblical insight is that *ubi Christus ibi ecclesia* (where Christ is, there is the Church).

Since it is on the basis of the experience of faith in the living Christ in the Christian communities of the South that we speak of the present shift, it also means that there is no *one* centre from which Christianity radiates, and it was never intended to be so. From this viewpoint, it would appear that the Lord's words: 'You will be witnesses for me in Jerusalem, in all Judaea and Samaria and to the ends of the earth' (Acts 1:8), were not intended to indicate a linear geographical progression of Christian history, meaning 'from Jerusalem, through Greece and Rome to Europe ... to the Third World through Europe' (Schumacher, 1974:213), for we cannot absolutise that pattern. Rather the Lord's words are to be taken as stressing the universality of the Gospel, conveyed in terms in which the disciples would have understood the world. The early chapters of the book of Acts indicate that the Jerusalem church was often overtaken by events, and the whole book can be read as the process whereby the early Christian leaders, predominantly Jewish, were brought to understand the mind of Christ which they had initially failed to grasp, as they inquired, 'Lord, will you at this time give the Kingdom back to Israel?' (Acts 1:6). Within the life-span of that early apostolic leadership, Jerusalem became 'periphery'. Yet the one apostle through whose ministry especially this came about, could anticipate that in the mercy of God, Jewry would again believe in Jesus the Messiah (Romans 9-11). So Jerusalem, where it all began, would need to believe again.

As with Jerusalem, so now, following the Western missionary penetration into the non-Western world, the Western world, 'a milieu that has become unchristian' (Rahner, 1974:32), needs to be re-evangelised. Indeed, we may say that it is precisely because the Western missionary enterprise has brought about the crumbling of the final vestiges of the notion of a territorial Christianity, namely, Western Christendom, that we now appreciate the nature of Christian history that seeks to approximate the mind of Christ. To that extent, the Western missionary endeavour has accomplished a feat comparable to St. Paul's, even though it may not always have used, if we are to believe Roland

Allen, St. Paul's methods (Allen, 1962).

If it was the Great Commission to make the Gospel available to the whole world that launched Christian history, it is legitimate to expect that all Christian history should be read in the light of the original impulse. The terms of the Great Commission ought to furnish us with the means of understanding and testing the direction and the major forces operating within any segment of Christian history. In our study of Christian history we should look for what the Great Commission teaches us to expect. In a helpful discussion of the subject, Walls has written: 'The words of the Great Commission [Matt. 28:19–20] require that the various nations are to be made disciples of Christ.' He draws attention to the fact that it is 'the *nations*, not some people within the nations, who are to be discipled'; and then he continues (Walls, 1990:25):

> In other words, national distinctions, the things that mark out each nation, the shared consciousness and shared traditions, and shared mental processes and patterns of relationship, are within the scope of discipleship. Christ can become visible within the very things which constitute nationality.

In his St. Colm's Lecture for 1989 (p.20), Walls related the subject to conversion:

> Conversion is not about adopting someone else's pattern of life and thought, however ancient and however excellent, that is not conversion but prose-lytisation...Conversion involves the turning towards Christ of everything that is there already, so that Christ comes into places, thoughts, relationships and world-views in which He has never lived before.

Applied to Christian history, the terms of the Great Commission calling for the 'discipling' and the 'conversion' of the nations, would lead to the realisation that no Christian history anywhere ceases to be a missionary history—a history of conversion, of the constant seeking and application of the mind of Christ to the issues and questions within a particular context, culture or nation—unless conversion has ceased to matter, or that seeking and applying the mind of Christ has ceased in that context, culture or nation. As an alternative to the dominant anthropology-based missiology that tends to reduce everything to the categories of 'the West and the rest', the whole of Christian history might be better read as mission history, and so made to yield from within it, clues to the queries and puzzles encountered elsewhere in the study of the Christian story. Missiology becomes not just learning to communicate the Gospel to other peoples and cultures, but also an exercise in self-understanding within Christian scholarship (Bediako, 1989).

If all Christian history is to be understood as missionary history—the application of the mind of Christ to, and in, context, conversion in context— the emergence of the 'new centres of Christianity's universality' makes our time perhaps the most exciting of all. For today no individual or individual church can speak the Word of God by itself alone, today also the universal Church resembles what it will look like at the end (according to the vision of Revelation 7) more than it has ever done. The promise of Pentecost has been fulfilled more abundantly than on the first day; and cross-cultural mission now comes into its own, for the whole Church has more opportunity to hear and share the Gospel as all of us 'hear in our own languages [contexts, cultures and nations] about the great things that God has done' (Acts 2:11).

The universal relevance of the Church's missionary histories in the Christian communities of the South comes, then, to consist in the extent to which those histories have been the histories of 'the great things that God has done'. This is also the answer to those Western Christian scholars who have doubted whether the cross-cultural missionary learning that has been gained within so-called 'pre-modern cultures' (of the South) can assist in mission to the 'modern Western world' (Newbigin, 1987). Has the modern Western world, in Christian recession, but with its increasing interest in the practice of the occult, so outgrown religious and spiritual hunger that it is impervious to the experiences of Christian transcendence recorded in the religious worlds of the South? What, then, is the significance of such cross-cultural missionary learning if it is shown to be truly of the Gospel?

The plurality of centres of Christianity's universality does not provide a linear unidirectional pattern of Christian history, but a pattern of overlapping circles of Christian life in context, with no absolute centres or peripheries. Every centre is a potential periphery and vice versa. Christian history in the post-missionary era brings Christians everywhere potentially into the experience of shared space for self-expression, the experience of community. I use the word 'potentially', for whilst such 'ecumenical sharing of resources' is a crucial pointer to the nature of Christian history itself, it requires a willingness to enter it and openness on all sides. To recall and paraphrase Mbiti's words: we have eaten theology with you ... will you eat theology with us?

Conclusion

At the 1978 Lambeth Conference, there were 80 bishops from Africa; in 1988 there were 175. In 1998, there were 226 (Conger, 1998). As the 1988 conference ended, an African bishop is reported to have commented: 'Anyone who wants a resolution passed in 1998 will have to come to terms with the African bishops' (Samuel and Sugden, 1989:4). Events show that that did indeed happen. Are Western bishops prepared to come to terms with that situation? The answer to that question is not simple or straightforward.

Our discussion has been about history, not prophecy. Yet prophecy itself is rooted in a judicious historical discernment concerning the things and the ways of God. For a puzzle which lies so evidently in the Christian future, we may look to Christian history and to the Christian Scriptures for guidance.

Towards the end of his long and profound letter to the Romans, in chapter 15, the seasoned apostle Paul suddenly turned to a subject that was obviously preoccupying him: his impending visit to Jerusalem to deliver gifts of money from the Gentile churches to the poor churches in Judaea. This was obviously important to the apostle, for he described it as being 'in the service of God's people there' (Romans 15:25). Paul was evidently pleased that the churches in Macedonia and Achaia had freely decided to give the offering, even though he was thoroughly convinced that the Gentiles had an obligation to help the Jews and that for a simple reason: 'Since the Jews shared their spiritual blessings with the Gentiles, the Gentiles ought to use their material blessings to help the Jews' (Romans 15:27).

If it was all so simple and straightforward, then what explains Paul's urgent request for prayer in vv. 30–32? Was Paul anxious lest the Jewish Christians, even in their evident need, should, in spiritual pride reject the gifts of their ill-rated Gentile brethren? If this were to happen, not only would it mean failure of an attempt to get resources from one group of Christians to another, but more importantly it would be a major setback for the Gospel. The whole operation had to do with God and Christ and the good news in an infinitely more profound way, as he had previously written to the Corinthians (2 Corinthians 9). A deeper insight into the apostle's mind on the present question is given us in Ephesians 2 & 3, for the passing of material gifts from the Gentiles to the Jews was the opportunity to demonstrate openly—before principalities and powers pulling in the opposite direction—the validity of the missionary proclamation of the Gospel, and the meaning of Christ as the clue to the design of God in history. This was to create, out of hostility, alienation and mutual suspicion, a new people, one people, the people of God with no wall separating them and keeping them enemies (Ephesians 2; 3:6).

It ought, then, to be through ecclesiastical historiography probing all Christian history as missionary history, as the history of the great things that God has done and is doing—contextual, intercontextual and trans-contextual—that the stubborn barriers that divide people behind the 'fetish' symbols of 'modern' and 'pre-modern', 'civilised' and 'uncivilised' are transcended and made to yield instead, the evidence of what God had been about since the foundation of the world.

The shape of Christian history in the age of the many new centres of Christianity's universality, therefore, offers the opportunity for all the different missionary histories to 'key into' the 'mainframe' of the one story of the enormous crowd that no one could number, from every race, tribe, nation and language. In their diverse tongues they stood in front of the throne of the Lamb and they all called out in one loud voice: 'Salvation comes from our God who sits on the throne, and from the Lamb' (Revelation 7:9-10).

References

Allen, Roland, 1962: *Missionary Methods—St. Paul's or Ours?* (Grand Rapids: Eerdmans; First published in 1912 by World Dominion Press).

Bediako, Kwame, 1989: 'World Evangelization, Institutional Evangelicalism and the future of Christian World Mission', in Vinay Samuel & Albrecht Hauser (eds), *Proclaiming Christ in Christ's Way—Studies in Integral Evangelism*, (Essays presented to Walter Arnold on his 60th birthday), (Oxford: Regnum Books), 52-68.

Boesak, Allan, 1984: *Black and Reformed—Apartheid, Liberation and the Calvinist Tradition*, (Johannesburg: Skotaville Publishers).

Boff, Leonardo, 1988: 'What are Third World Theologies?', in Leonardo Boff & Vergilio Elizondo (eds), *Third World Theologies—Convergences and Differences,* (Concilium 199),(Edinburgh: T. & T. Clark).

Conger, George, 1998: *Lambeth Directory: The Worldwide Anglican Communion 1998*, (Carlisle: Oxford Centre for Mission Studies/American Anglican Council).

Gutterrez, Gustavo, 1973: *A Theology of Liberation—History, Politics and Salvation,* (New York: Orbis Books; first published in Spanish in 1971).

– 1983: *We drink from our own wells,* (New York: Orbis Books, ET 1984).

Mbiti, John, 1976: 'Theological impotence and the universality of the Church' in Gerald H. Anderson, & Thomas F. Stransky (eds), *Mission Trends No. 3: Third World Theologies,* (New York: Paulist Press; Grand Rapids: Eerdmans, 6-18. First published in Lutheran World, XXI/3, 1974).

Mveng, Engelbert, 1988: 'African Liberation Theology', in Boff & Elizondo (eds), *Third World Theologies*, 15-27.

Newbigin, Lesslie, 1987: 'Can the West be converted?', in *International Bulletin of Missionary Research*, vol 11/1, January, (1987), 2-7.

Pieris, Aloysius, 1988: *Towards an Asian Theology of Liberation*, (New York: Orbis Books; Edinburgh: T. & T. Clark).

Rahner, Karl, 1974: *The Shape of the Church to come*, (London: SPCK).

Rayan, Samuel, 1988: 'Third World theology: where do we go from here?', in Boff & Elizondo (eds), *Third World Theologies*.

Samuel, Vinay & Sugden, Chris (eds), 1984: *Sharing Jesus in the Two-Thirds World*, Grand Rapids: Eerdmans, viii. (First published, in 1983 in Bangalore, India, by Partnership in Mission (PIM)-Asia.)

– 1989: *Lambeth: A View from the Two-Thirds World*, (London: SPCK).

Schumacher, John, 1974: 'The Third World and the Twentieth Century Church', in Gerald H. Anderson & Thomas F. Stransky (eds), *Mission Trends No. I: Crucial Issues in Mission Today*, (New York: Paulist Press; Grand Rapids: Eerdmans, 205-14. First published in *Concilium*, September 1971).

Torres, Sergio, & Fabella, Virginia (eds), 1978: *The Emergent Gospel—Theology from the Developing World*, (London: G. Chapman).

Torres, S., 1988: 'Dar-es-Salaam 1976' in Boff & Elizondo (eds), *Third World Theologies*.

Walls, Andrew F., 1987: 'The Christian tradition in Today's World', in F.B. Whaling (ed.), *Religion in Today's World*, (Edinburgh: T. & T. Clark), 76-109.

– 1989: *The significance of Christianity in Africa*, (Edinburgh: Church of Scotland/St. Colm's Education Centre and College).

– 1990: 'The translation principle in Christian history', in Stine, Philip C. (ed.) *Bible Translation and the Spread of the Church—The last 200 hundred years* (Studies in Christian Mission 2), (Leiden: EJ Brill), 24-39.

CHAPTER 10

Publications of Kwame Bediako

1980   'The Willowbank Consultation, January 1978—a personal reflection', *Theme-lios, an international journal for theological students,* Vol.5, No.2, January (1980), 25-32.

1984   'Biblical Christologies in the context of African Traditional Religion', in Vinay Samuel and Chris Sugden (eds.), *Sharing Jesus in the Two-Thirds World,* (Grand Rapids: Eerdmans, 1984), 81-121.

1985   'The missionary inheritance', in Robin Keeley (ed.), *Christianity: A world faith,* (Tring: Lion Publishing, 1985), 303-11.

1986   'The Holy Spirit, the Christian Gospel and religious change: the African evidence for a Christian theology of religious pluralism', in James Thrower (ed.), *Essays in Religious Studies for Andrew Walls,* (Aberdeen: Dept. of Religious Studies, University of Aberdeen, 1986), 44-56.

'Christian tradition and the African God revisited: a process in the exploration of a theological idiom', in David Gitari and Patrick Benson (eds.), *Witnessing to the Living God in contemporary Africa,* (Nairobi: Uzima Press, 1986), 77-97.

1988   Articles on 'African Christian Theology', 'Theology of African Independent Churches', 'Culture' and 'Black Theology', *New Dictionary of Theology,* (Leicester, England/Downers Grove, USA: IVP, 1988).

'Christ in Africa: some reflections on the contribution of Christianity to the African becoming', in Christopher Fyfe (ed.), *African Futures,* (25th Anniversary Conference, Seminar Proceedings No.28), (Edinburgh: Centre of African Studies, 1988), 447-58.

1989   'The roots of African Theology', *International Bulletin of Missionary Research,* Vol. 13, No. 2, April (1989), 58-65.

'Into all the world', in Richard Bauckham et al. (eds.), *Jesus 2000,* (Oxford: Lion Publishing, 1989), 222-25.

1989   'World evangelisation, institutional evangelicalism and the future of the Christian world mission', in V. Samuel and A. Hauser (eds.), *Proclaiming Christ in Christ's way—Studies in integral evangelism* (Essays presented to Walter Arnold on the occasion of his 60th birthday), (Oxford: Regnum Books, 1989), 52-68.

1990   *Jesus in African culture—a Ghanaian perspective, (*Accra: Asempa Publishers, 1990); reprinted 1992.

1992   *Theology and Identity: the impact of culture on Christian thought in the second century and modern Africa, (*Oxford: Regnum Books, 1992). (This book was selected as a finalist for the 1993 Harper-Collins Religious Book Award); reprinted 1999.

'New paradigms on ecumenical co-operation: An African perspective', *International Review of Mission,* July (1992), 375-79.

'The relevance of a Christian approach to culture in Africa', in *Christian Education in the African Context,* (Proceedings of the first Africa regional conference of the International Association for the Promotion of Christian Higher Education —IAPCHE—held in Harare, Zimbabwe, 4-9 March 1991), (Grand Rapids: IAPCHE, 1992), 24-35.

1993   'Unmasking the powers—Christianity, Authority and Desacralisation in modern African politics', in John Witte (ed.), *Christianity and Democracy in Global Context, (*Boulder: Westview Press, 1993), 207-30.

'Cry Jesus! Christian Theology and Presence in Modern Africa', *Vox Evangelica,* Vol. XXIII, April (1993), 7-25.

'John Mbiti's contribution to African Theology', in Jacob Olupona and Sulayman S. Nyang (eds.), *Religious Plurality in Africa: Essays in honour of John S. Mbiti, (*Berlin: Mouton de Gruyter, 1993), 367-90.

1994   'The impact of the Bible in Africa', Epilogue in Ype Schaaf, *On their way rejoicing—The history and role of the Bible in Africa, (*Carlisle: Paternoster Press, 1994), 243-54.

'Understanding African Theology in the twentieth century', *Themelios,* Vol. 20, No. 1, October (1994), 14-19.

'Christ is Lord! How is Jesus Christ unique in the midst of other faiths?', *Trinity Journal of Church and Theology,* (Legon), vol. 14, no. 2, (Dec. 1994–Jan 1995), 50-61.

1995   'The significance of modern African Christianity—A Manifesto', *Studies in World Christianity (The Edinburgh Review of Theology and Religion),* vol. 1, no.1, (1995), 51-67.

'De-sacralisation and Democratisation—Some theological reflections on the role of Christianity in nation-building in modern Africa', *Transformation*, Vol. 12, No. 1, January-March (1995), 1-4.

'Theologie van het grondvlak—Afrika en de toekomst van het christendom', *Wereld en Zending*, 24ste Jaargang, 2, (1995), 27-39.

Christianity in Africa—The Renewal of a Non-Western Religion, (Edinburgh/ New York: Edinburgh University Press/Orbis Books, 1995; reprinted 1997).

1996 'How is Jesus Christ Lord?—Aspects of an Evangelical Christian Apologetics in the context of African religious pluralism', *Exchange*, Vol. 25, No. 1, (1996), 27-42.

'Proclaiming Christ today—as an African and Evangelical Christian', in Huibert van Beek & Georges Lemopoulos (eds.), *Proclaiming Christ Today*, (Orthodox-Evangelical Consultation, Alexandria, 10-15 July 1995), (Geneva: WCC/Bialystok, Poland: Syndesmos, 1996), 30-43.

'Five theses on the significance of modern African Christianity: A Manifesto', *Transformation*, Vol. 13, No. 1, January/March (1996), 20-29. [An expanded version of the article published in *Studies in World Christianity, (The Edinburgh Review of Theology and Religion)*, vol. 1, no.1, (1995), 51-67.]

'Understanding African theology in the 20th century', *Bulletin for Contextual Theology in Southern Africa and Africa,* Vol. 3, No. 2, June (1996), 1-11.

'African Theology', in David Ford (ed.), *The Modern Theologians* (second edition), (Oxford: Basil Blackwell, 1996), 426-44.

'Theological Reflections', in Yamamori et al. (eds.), *Serving with the Poor in Africa*, (Monrovia: MARC, 1996), 181-92.

1997 'What is the Gospel?', *Transformation*, Vol.14, No.1, Jan/March (1997), 1-4.

'Johannes Christaller', 'Clement Anderson Akrofi', 'Ephraim Amu', 'William Ofori-Atta', in Gerald H. Anderson (ed.), *Biographical Dictionary of Christian Missions*, (New York: Macmillan, 1997).

1998 'Facing the Challenge: Africa in World Christianity in the 21st century—A vision of the African Christian future', *Journal of African Christian Thought*, Vol. 1, No. 1, June (1998), 52-57.

'The Doctrine of Christ and the Significance of Vernacular Terminology', *International Bulletin of Missionary Research,* Vol. 22, No. 3, July (1998), 110-11.

1999   *Jezus in de cultuur en geschiedenis van Afrika*, (Kampen: Uitgeverij Kok Kampen).

Forthcoming in 2000:

'African Christian Thought', and 'John Mbiti', in Adrian Hastings (ed.), *Oxford Companion of Christian Thought*, (Oxford: OUP).

Regnum Studies in Mission

(Uniform with this Volume)

Theology and Identity
*The Impact of Culture upon Christian Thought
in the Second Century and in Modern Africa*
Kwame Bediako

The author examines the question of Christian identity in the context of the Graeco–Roman culture of the early Roman Empire. He then addresses the modern African predicament of quests for identity and integration.

1992 / 1-870345-10-X / 518pp

Paradigm Wars
*The Southern Baptist International Mission Board
Faces the Third Millennium*
Keith E Eitel

The International Mission Board of the Southern Baptist Convention is the largest denominational mission agency in North America. This volume chronicles the historic and contemporary forces that led to the IMB's recent extensive reorganization, providing the most comprehensive case study to date of a historic mission agency restructuring to continue its mission purpose into the 21st century more effectively.

1999 / 1-870345-12-6 / 150pp

Dalit Consciousness and Christian Conversion
Historical Resources for a Contemporary Debate
(Published jointly with ISPCK)
Samuel Jayakumar

The main focus of this historical study is social change and transformation among the Dalit Christian communities in India. Historiography tests the evidence in the light of the conclusions of the modern Dalit liberation theologians.

1999 / 1-870345-31-2 / 457pp

Seeking the Asian Face of Jesus
*The Practice and Theology of Christian Social Witness
in India and Indonesia 1974–1996*
Christopher Sugden

Contemporary wholistic mission with the poor in India and Indonesia combining the call to transformation of all life in Christ with micro-credit enterprise schemes. 'The literature on contextual theology now has a new standard to rise to' – *Lamin Sanneh (Yale University, USA)*.

1997 / 1-870345-26-6 / 518pp

Gospel, Culture and Transformation
A Reprint, with a New Introduction, of Part Two of
Seeking the Asian Face of Jesus
Christopher Sugden

Gospel, Culture and Transformation explores the practice of mission especially in relation to transforming cultures and communities. Vinay Samuel has played a leading role in developing the understanding of mission as transformation, which he defines as follows: 'Transformation is to enable God's vision of society to be actualised in all relationships: social, economic and spiritual, so that God's will may be reflected in human society and his love experienced by all communities, especially the poor.'

2000 / 1-870345-32-0 / 160pp approx

Mangoes or Bananas?
The Quest for an Authentic Asian Christian Theology
Hwa Yung

Asian Christian thought remains largely captive to Greek dualism and enlightenment rationalism because of the overwhelming dominance of Western culture. Authentic contextual Christian theologies will emerge within Asian Christianity with a dual recovery of confidence in culture and the gospel.

1997/1-870345-25-8 / 285pp

Regnum Books International
P O Box 300
Carlisle Cumbria
CA3 0QS UK

Web: www.paternoster-publishing.com